Wolves of the Sapphire Sun

Wolves of The Sapphire Sun

VUUHJNUH

by

C. JoyBell C.

The inscriptions on the title page are of the language *Malachim,* which is widely accepted amongst mystic scholars to be the most extant historical remnant intact today, of the writing and language mode of Angelic Beings. The use of this writing is documented in archaic manuscripts dating back to the reign of King Solomon in Israel, (est. 970 to 931 BC.) Even more ancient evidence of this writing is available in even more olden manuscripts dating back to centuries prior to the era of King Solomon. Please treat the *Malachim* writings with respect. Please do not write on top of it, add to it, and please take care not to damage the page whereon it is written. The letters herein spell out a protective utterance used to shield one from all attacks of enemies.

Copyright © 2014 C. JoyBell C.
All rights reserved.

All books by C. JoyBell C. are printed in the U.S.A., Great Britain and Continental Europe.

ISBN: **1494979799**
ISBN- **978-1494979799**

This book may not be reproduced in whole or in part by any electronic or mechanical means including photocopying and the use of information storage and retrieval systems, without permission in writing from the copyright owner. No derivative works or adaptations may be produced without prior written consent from the copyright owner. Excerpts and quotations are allowed for non-commercial purposes, where clear reference to the author is given.

www.cjoybellc.com
authorcjoybellc@gmail.com

This one's for the wild ones. ♡

— C. JoyBell C.

Introduction

Welcome to the pages of my wildest book, to-date! It didn't start out this wild, though! When I first began this venture, it was intended to be a book of poetry for children and when you begin reading the first pages, my bet is that you'll pick up on that vibe, exactly. It opens gently, softly, slightly amusing here and there… you will feel like an insightful, thoughtful child reading the beginning pages. As you progress on this discovery though, that feeling will wear off, just how my intentions to make this into a children's book, wore off! As I delved into writing this collection of poetry, my intentions evolved and it was no longer going to be specifically for children. I could picture the book becoming a great source of comfort for those who feel like they are different in otherworldly, supernatural ways. And then, envisioning my book of poetry as a collective story, I started stringing the poems together to form a novel-made-out-of-poems! I realized that it was all about a few characters and their stories (include me in as one of those characters), intermingling. I have given the life in the main voice of this book to the character I have named *Filippa*, while the wolf I have written into a character I call, *Ezekiel*. The idea isn't to convey that every poem is about either of them, rather, I want you to understand that they are the named embodiments of the voices in these poems. I see this as the same characters moving through different lifetimes, different dimensions— always bound to each other.

What I really appreciate about producing a book of poetry within the concept of a short novel— is that this approaches the novel from a non-constrictive point of view! It's a novel but then the novel part is incorporeal. The novel is the soul while the physical body (corporeal) is the poetry. You are allowed to think as you wish, feel as you wish! The possibilities are truly endless! And what can I say? I *love* creating endless things!

Nearing the end of the manuscript, I tapped into my sensuous, erotic inclinations and as you will see, have come out with the most explicit erotica in the history of my career as an author! I sincerely do not want my mother or aunties to read this book. Haha! Altogether, I believe that I have created something very human in that it evolves in a growth process similar to the human body: child, adolescent and adult. I can also feel that I have woven together a self-indulgent story-novel-poetrybook which has been pieced together quite wonderfully, if I may say so myself. The entire book does feel more like a short novel than a collection of poems.

By the end of your read, you should feel that you have reached a climax that is encompassing and satisfying, while not answering every single question you may have been led to ask yourself while you were reading the book; because those questions raised are the wolves that will continue to relentlessly dig into the soil and snow of your mind and plant seeds in your heart, long after you've already finished reading!

You might be wondering, *why Wolves of the Sapphire Sun? Why not Wolves of the Sapphire Moon?* And initially that thought crossed my mind, too. Moon would make more sense since that would translate to a Blue Moon, Wolves of the Blue Moon. But try as I might, I just couldn't get the *Sun* out of my title! Then it dawned on me that if I couldn't get it out of there— then that definitely meant it was supposed to be there! I recalled my previous works, *The Sun Is Snowing* and *The Suns Snow And The Sands Move,* when it occurred to me that I've never produced anything just because it "makes more sense." In fact, everything I write and do, redefines what "makes more sense" is supposed to mean! Since when did Suns start to snow, anyway? Since I made them snow! And there you have it! Sapphire Sun it is! You might also be wondering, *why wolves?* Well, I don't know for sure. All I know is that there is a wolf in my dreams at night, he watches over me, and sometimes we run together!

Every time I write a book, I feel like it's my most revealing work, ever. Until I write another one and can see that I have again created a "most revealing work, ever." This book though, is work that I have fallen absolutely in love with, as I feel like my fingerprints are all over it! I am, for the first time, truly speechless about how it is I feel towards this particular work of mine. Language escapes me. Perchance I could have said the same thing about all my other books; but every time I fall in love with something I have created, it's a new love all over again and in new love, new things are found! In this book in particular, I can tell you that the things to be found are wild, unbound, dirty, secret, serene, sacred, sin-like, and breathtaking! I will be thrilled to hear you flip through these pages... remember that you are not alone, those of "our kind" are always with you...

"Thou hast drunk of the fountain of divine light, with undefiled heart hast thou penetrated into the inmost mysteries. The solemn hour has come for me to bring thee to the very fountain of life and light. Those who have not removed the dense veil which conceals invisible wonders from men's eyes have not become sons of the Gods.

Listen now to truths, which must not be told the mass of mortals, truths which give might to the sanctuaries."

~ Orpheus

Melted Vanilla

She had a little basket
Where she kept her
Many, little things
He liked to watch her in the sunlight
While it flew in
Through the window
And bent itself around her skin
As she stood over her basket
Set on the breakfast nook

She always sat it on the breakfast nook

He liked to watch her because
Never before had he seen someone
Cry like she did
Silken tears rolling down her cheeks
Gently and smoothly like melted vanilla
When she picked up some small things that
Made her a little sad
Like a broken robin's egg
"I wonder what happened to the baby bird"
She would whisper to herself
While the melted vanilla trickled
Down her cheeks

C. JoyBell C.

"But maybe it just hatched
And flew away" he would say
Then she would smile
So suddenly
And her smile would light up
Inside her eyes like
Lightning bugs
And she would laugh even!
Like the sunshine was tickling her
While it swam over the freckles
Scattered over her shoulders

She filled her basket with small things
Like broken robins' eggs
And little lost feathers

Beautiful Freak

When I was little
I used to sit under the sunlight
And grow flowers out of my hands
First the petals would show their colors
Then the stem would slowly rise to the surface
Then the leaves would gently unfurl
Reaching for the sky!

When I was little
I grew flowers out of my hands
I wanted to share them with people
But when I showed them to the people
They didn't want them!
They got scared!
And I didn't know where to go…

So I walked alone
They threw stones at me and rocks at me
They poked me with sticks
And sometimes they pulled my hair
They called me a freak, a weirdo
For growing flowers from
My palms

I kept on walking alone
For a long time I did

C. JoyBell C.

Until one day I saw the most beautiful creature
I'd ever seen
She grew a rose from the palm of her hand
Right in front of my eyes!
And then she gave it to me

I could grow the same kind of rose, too!
And I could grow it in different colors
If I wanted to!
I was just like her! I was beautiful, too!
And then I knew I never, ever walked alone!
There are many of us
We are just too beautiful

That's why most people can't see us

It's Okay They Didn't Want Me

At first I was sad
Because in the big, big building
Filled with lots of white apartments
They all wanted to stay in one apartment
Without me
They said mine was at the other end of the hallway
So I would be alone
All alone in my own apartment
And that made me sad

Outside the building of white apartments
I found a baby eagle
It had a leather string attached to its talon
And it let me pick it up
Its wings were something
Like butterfly wings
With symbols inscribed into them
I liked watching the sunlight
Filter through the symbols
They were like holes in its wings!

I took the baby eagle to my family in their apartment
But they didn't want the eagle, either!
They said the eagle had to stay away
With me in my own place
So I walked down the hallways
I found my own door
I don't remember the number
But I found it.

C. JoyBell C.

It was a small room
And I was all alone with my eagle
But a friend of mine dropped by
I don't really know her
But in my dream she was my friend
She said
"It's not too bad"
And
"Look outside the windows"
So I pulled the curtains back
GASP!
Outside my window, I had a big, big lawn!
A lawn with overgrown grass
And big, beautiful white and pink tulips
In v-shaped vases hanging on
The short iron fence that marked my territory
At first I thought it was a terrace
Or a balcony
But then I looked and I saw
It was part of a whole land!
And the fenced-in part was mine!
ALL MINE!
Then I looked beyond and saw
I was at the edge of a mountain!
And below me there was an ocean,
A great-blue sea!
In front of me there were godlike mountains
That touched the clouds
And overlooked the water!
The tulips all around my lawn
Were soooooooo beautiful!
And the horses— yes there were horses!
The horses leaped in over the iron fence
And roamed on my grass that blew in the wind!

The mountains beyond and the ocean below!
The fjords to either side!
The ponies and the tulips
The wind that blew the grass
ALL was MINE
Just mine and my eagle's
Then I thought
It was okay
That they didn't want me to stay with them
In their apartment
At the other side
Of the hall

C. JoyBell C.

Little Filippa

She was born with a rose
Etched into the palm of her hand
That's why whenever she saw
Roses
She would reach out to touch them
Because her skin would
Call out to be reunited
We would be sitting in McDonald's
Eating burgers and fries
She would reach out to touch
The roses wrapped in crepe paper
In the flower shoppe display
Right beside the McDonald's store
She would walk over to the flower stand
Just to touch the roses
What on earth are you doing?
I would ask her
She would say
That the rose was given to her
By her father
So that she would never forget
Where she had come from
So that she would always have
A way to touch home
And to call herself back home
And to hear the loving voices
That called out her name
Reminding her that she belonged to them
And not to us down here

Of course it was a very strange thing
To say
And I warned her not to tell anyone else
What she had told me
But then she said there was another one
Just like her
And that her father called to him
Too, because they were both
From the same place, both of them, together
And I asked her if he had a rose in his palm
Just like hers
She told me that the rose was only hers
And that he had something else
He had a song
A wild call
In the palm of his hand
He would hold out his hand into
The winds and the storms
So the call would
Answer the winds
So the song would
Echo the storms
And he would remember his home, too
What does a rose really mean?
I asked her one day at the mall
It is the one thing that's not from here
But that's a hundred percent from above
She told me
But they grow from the ground
I said to her
They do, just like I was born here, too
But just like me, it's from above
It's not from here, at all

Little Filippa (2)

"Did you know that the rose
Never does die?"
It was s starry, starry night
And her eye caught the sparkle
Of Orion's Belt
I asked her what she meant
Couldn't she see that petals fall
That leaves wither
That the vibrant colors fade away?
"All of that is only as you see it to be"
She said to me
"The petals fall not, they lose not their color
They die not
It is only your eyes that see this"
I asked her how she could say
Such a thing
When clearly the rose petals
Did all of that and
Returned to the dust of the earth
"You see it that way with your eyes
Because your eyes were taught
To believe in death
So when it is about the time of the rose
To die
In your eyes
Your soul begins to make it fade away
It's only what you know, that's what you see
But it's not really gone, a rose never
Ever dies

Because it is from above!"
She pointed up at Lynx, Cygnus and Andromeda
I asked her how she could talk
So crazy like that
When all can see
That a rose returns to the dust
A lily returns to the dust
People do, too…
"It's only happening in this little place
In your eyes
Where your soul makes
A little hiding place for dead things"
She told me
"But if you were to take that hiding place
Away
If you were to make it into
A glasshouse, instead
Then you wouldn't see the petals rot
You wouldn't see the colors fade
And fall, mix with the dust
You would see it as it is
The rose is eternal"
She said to me
We were munching on caramel popcorn
That starry, starry night

Where's God?

Sometimes I wonder
If someone stole God
From Heaven

When I look into the mirror
Some days

I actually *see* it

When I can't find my smile
In the mirror
I think it

Astronomer

I'm an astronomer
Because I look up into the sky
And study the things
That are in it

But maybe I used to be
And earthonomer
Because perhaps I lived
On Alcyone in Pleiades
And with a big telescope
I searched for earth!

You're on earth!

And since you're here
I think
Maybe that's why I'm
Here now
I found you on my telescope
On the way down to earth
Riding on the back
Of a falling star
That landed somewhere
And made a big hole in the crust!

C. JoyBell C.

So maybe I
Was an earthonomer
Because of you
And now I'm an astronomer
So we can go back one day
To where we came from

Or maybe it's the whole other way
Around
Maybe you're the earthonomer
And I study the sky now
Because I want to go home one day
After all
I just fell down
And you're only here
Because I'm fallen

Either way

You're with me

This Is What I Think of You

Space diamonds are formed when
Stardust explodes into the universe
And those dusts collide with each other
At speeds of more than
Ten thousand miles per hour
But not all collisions make space diamonds
If they slam into each other hard enough
They would only destroy one another
And if they run into each other a little
Too slowly, then diamonds aren't born
So it has to be perfect.
Everything has to be perfect.
And maybe, just maybe
The universe has to be a perfect shade of
Midnight blue for it to happen
And maybe the galaxies around
Need to have their planets in alignment
Who knows, the sun and the moon
Might need to kiss each other at the same time
That the stardust collides
To create a space diamond
Here's the thing
I think that you're made up of
Space diamonds
Lots and lots
And lots of them

C. JoyBell C.

I Guess That's Okay

Today it was windy outside
I pulled up a chair, sat in the garden
The vines on the fence were
Flailing, in and out of the fence holes
Their purple flowers
Were being tossed back and forth
A blue butterfly fluttered by
It lingered for a minute
Around my face, it fluttered around
And around my face
Making me smile
The sunlight shone through its wings
And that made me smile, too
But then I looked closer…
The wind slowed down and the blue thing
Dropped lower, down towards the ground
It slowed down in the sunbeam
Almost stopped fluttering around
And that's when I saw that
It wasn't a butterfly, at all!
It was a piece of blue paper!
A tiny piece of blue paper!
But I thought it was a butterfly the whole time!
And it made me smile, just like
A butterfly can make anyone smile!
Especially a blue one!
So I thought that, maybe,
Even if you're not everything I thought you were
That's okay because
At least you made me smile…

Big

Poems are
Little stories
With BIG hearts

Or maybe their hearts
Are average sized
Just like any others' hearts

But since the poems themselves
Are so very little
That makes their hearts look BIG

Poems are little things
With hearts too big
For them to handle

And that's why
People like poems
Because

Poems are like people!
Too much of the time
Their hearts are

Too big for them to handle!

Another Planet

There is a place
Where the weather happens in the water
You stand beside the flowing waters
And watch
The weathers of your life
Emerge and submerge
The blankets you once slept under
The toys you used to play with
Everything is in those waters!
The stream changes colors
Like the sky does
From dark to light
From grey to blue
Like the seasons changing
Stirred by all the things
You thought were forgotten!
Everything is still there!
If you could just go
And stand beside the stream
Like I did
You would see everything all over again!
Floating and swimming
In the sky of the stream
It is another planet maybe
Or another dimension, for sure!
There is a sky there, too

The clouds run across
Fast and then slow
And fast again!
You'll see mountains that appear
Then disappear
Behind the fast clouds
That grow and dance
Faster and faster

I guess you can say
That they have two skies
One up there
And one below, in the waters
I guess that means
Both ways are up!
Up is up
But down is up, too!

I like that planet

Anchor

She is a little broken.
When something hurts in her heart
She leaves it behind
Along with everything in it
Sails away on the waves of her mind
To get far away from herself
As far as far can be!

But he's there in the middle
Of her sailing mind
And her forgotten heart
Because he is in her dreams at night
The place where
The heart and mind meet
That's where he goes

He is the one
She can never leave behind
He calls out her name
While she sails out on her ship
And she returns.
He is the one who
Holds the anchor

Outside-In

They always taught me
To let things go
Put the bird back in the tree
Let the butterfly out

Freedom

But I think I want
A different kind of freedom
Someone to keep me
And then *keep me free*
Inside their heart!

Because I feel like

A heart is the best place
To run around in
Or
To fly around in!
Better than the sky
Or

A big tree!

So I want to be
The butterfly that flutters
Its wings inside someone's heart

So I want to be
The bird that escapes
From the outside, into one's soul!

I want freedom from the outside-in

Sandcastles

Every day on the seashore
He built a castle of sand for her
The little grains glistened in the light
Of day
And were so golden glowing
It's almost like they reflected
The waves
And even captured the smell of the seas
Inside their
Little, tiny, sandy hearts

But it was very sad

Because he built a castle for her
Every day
But she tore it down
Every night
For a little while it would make her happy
And she smiled to watch his hands
Building the castles for her
But then when evening fell
And the shadows crawled
Along the shoreline
She would get scared
Of losing her castles
Of losing everything
To the night
So every twilight
As the sun went down and cast
Beautiful colors across the sky

She would tear down the castle
While he watched and cried
"Stop!" He would say
"It took me a long time!"
But she'd rather her own hands
Break it
Than it be taken away by the dark

But it was also very beautiful

Because every morning
He was there again
Rebuilding the castle all over again
Making her laugh
Watching her smile
Handful of sand upon handful
Shovel after shovel
Even if he knew
It would be torn down
As the day ended
He still went back every morning
To build castles for her
Out of beautiful sand
From dawn to dusk

And every night at bedtime
As her head lay down to sleep
She always thought he
Would never come back
But she was wrong
Every time
Because the next day

There he was again

C. JoyBell C.

My Rose

On the other side of the lake, there can be found
a hundred thousand roses. But here with me now I
have one beautiful rose that makes me happy with its
sweet scent and soft petals. It is mine and I
will keep it. I want to see the amazingness, the sweetness
in what I do have; rather than see the sweetness
that I can't have yet. One day I will sail on my boat to the
other side of the lake and when I get there I will have not
only one rose, not only a hundred thousand roses, but I will
have a hundred thousand and one.

Half Witch

I don't know what's so wrong
With being half witch
It's a beautiful thing
I can make roses
Grow out of my hands
And I can
Listen to the heartbeats
Of the colored stones
And hear a still small voice
In the winds
But you can hear the voice, too!
Even if you're not half witch!
Because the voice is for everyone
You just have to listen

And I don't know why they
Say bad things about us witches

I picked up a dying bird the other day
A small sparrow
And it came back to life
In my hands

It's not a bad thing

Emerald

My heart must be made of
Emerald
For the color does not fade

My heart must be made of
Ruby
For the blood is true

My heart must be made of
Sapphire
For in it is found the sky

My heart must be made of
Diamond
For they cannot break it

Hearts and Stones

It is because my heart
Fell into the river one day
And was carried away
By the dirty water
That's why they came
To give me a heart
Made of gold
And it's because
My heart was smashed
One night in my sleep
It was torn from my body
That's why they came to me
And placed a ruby in my chest
And it's really because
My heart was numbed
By the pins
Stuck into it
That's why they came
To place a diamond within me
A fire within me
A furnace within me
A sapphire soul have I
So I cannot hate
So I must forgive
Because to me is given back
More hearts more valuable

Than the one I had before

Archangel

In her
Flows the blood of Archangels
For the blood of the Angels
Does not run thin
Does not dry out
Does not wash away
Does not dilute, dissolve, disband
A single drop
Is all it takes
To revive a legion
And from her
The legion will be awakened
By her footsteps
The stones will breathe again
Her passing by
Will wake the boulders
And the mountains
She will unite Mercury and Venus
For in her veins runs thick
The blood of Raziel and Gabriel
Metatron and Michael

C. JoyBell C.

Next Time

Beyond the war-torn fields
Where humans kill and wound
One another
There lies a great expanse
Of lavenders and lilacs
Covered in grey haze

I stepped beyond our world of chaos
And into the grey mists
Where satyrs roamed
And nymphs played with one another
I've been here before

Familiar but new
This place
Hesitant yet compelled
Was I
Their eyes glistened the way that
Mine do

Their skin translucent
The way that mine is

It felt like things that
Teachers and preachers
Tell you to stay away from
And yet it felt like home!

"Why don't you ever go out there?"
I asked

"Look at their hearts— always changing,
It frightens us!"
I was told

"What about my heart,
What is it like?"
I stood in front of the fawn
And he stood to the same exact
Stature as I did
We looked eye-to-eye
"Your heart is human
But it is naked, all naked."
He said to me
"Not like theirs."

I wanted to roam further
And deeper
Into the lavender haze
But I hesitated

Next time
I won't stop
I will go further

Wolf

There they are
Your eyes, always your eyes
Piercing through the barriers of time and space
Cutting through the jagged air
Your stare
Grey and green
A wolf's eyes
From every angle
I am surrounded
From century to century to century
There they are!
There you are
My wolf
Always and always
You have never left me
And I can't see you
But I know you
And I can't hold you
But you hold me in the winds
You know me
Better than they do
Better than I do
And I think I know you too
I think I look at you too
When I feel you pull me in
That's you

And they've always said
My eyes can burn
That's because
I'm a wolf too
We are the same

I wait for you

Wolf (2)

She could see through his eyes
And he could see through hers
No matter
Where in this world they were
A hundred million miles apart
They shared a single wind
They shared a single soul
So wherever her wolf roamed
She roamed with him, too
Through his eyes
She saw the cliffs
The forests and the skies
And wherever she was
He was with her too
Through her eyes
He saw the fireplace
The single bed
Her lonely walls
And on their shared wind
He would sail in at midnight
Through her open window
Why would she leave it open?
Only a little, just for him
She felt
Something always came at night

For her
To watch her sleeping
To feel her breath
On its face
So she kept the window open
Just a little

Wolves

They wonder
Always wonder
Why she gravitates t'wards
The lone wolves
Why she
Finds so much solace
In the untameables
The hungry ones
The wandering ones
The ones carrying
Meanderings and plights
Of the embattled soul
She wonders sometimes, too
Why can't she
Find home with
The quiet ones
The ones found
And not lost
The wild ones encircle her
Mark her as their own
As home
As the place
To come home to
She alone
Holds the scent
She is marked
The only female of her kind
Her spirit calls out
To the one
Who has never really left her

Amaranthine

I found something
Undying, eternal
Poking up from
Under the ground
It caught my eye
As I walked alone
Down that path
While I stood there
Waiting for you
Did you put it there?
Did you bury it there
Under the ground?
So I uncovered it
From the dirt
And mangled tree roots
It was dark and purple
It felt like velvet
But looked like glass
Fumes escaped
And raped my eyes
Colored in my irises with the
Tincture of itself, and
Left your signature
Upon my soul
Is this the ink that you write with?
Words into our wind?

C. JoyBell C.

Is this a letter from you?
Released by fumes
Poisoning my spirit
With a sweet venom
Saying you'll always be there…

Tears of Joy

I am here
Crying and smiling
In the darkness of this room
I cry tears of joy
And my skin quivers
Under the breath of God
I am so near, I am so near
I am here
Under the breath of God
And my very flesh quivers
I cry tears of joy
The happiness of the Hierarchies
Spell my name, flowing down
My face
I am here, It is done
What is done?
I don't know
But then I am sure of it
I cry tears of joy
Over a happiness
I have yet to name!
Before I have touched it
I have already touched it
Before I have tasted
I have already tasted

And I thought I knew what
A sweet vision sounded like
I thought I knew well
The sweet picture of a love
Until the gods said,
"No, even that was not enough"
They say,
"Let Us write Our Names
And the names of Angels
On Your face
Let Us take You home to Us

The Temple and The Sun

Spells

I heard them talking
Through that crack in the wall

From the other room
Their hushed voices

Like airborne incense escaped
To my ears

They sang soft songs
Of great birds, eagles

They hummed gentle tunes
Of salamanders and sylphs

Spells

Incantations

I was there every
Day at noontime

Thought maybe I could
One day discover a hex

To bring me back to you

Stone

They say you are cold to the touch
And harsh on the eyes
Yet as the soles of my feet pass over you
Shuffling, creating small clouds of dust
For me to walk on
And as I pass my fingertips
Over your surface
Passing like transgressions
Over your calloused covering
Somehow I feel that my skin is made
Of the same binding
And I feel like
I have made mad, mad love
On these steps before
That I have made mad, mad love
Between these stone walls before
I have worshipped, lit sanctified fires
I have glowed in the flames
Spun for God
Everywhere my feet step
All ground I touch
Is become a stone temple
My own shadows from eternity
Stand beside me
Reflected on the surface
Of your uneven finish
I can see where the chisels honed you
I can feel where
You were pulled from the mountainsides

They say you are cold to the touch
And yet here
In between your walls
Under your archways
Above your roughened floors
Sand and dirt
Cling to my feet
And I am not cold
You feel as smooth to me
As the sensation of my own skin
You remind me of as many
Burning thoughts
As my own mind can contain
They have told me that
The stones have spirits, souls
Indeed you have a spirit
That screams and glances
A soul that
Feasts and leaps

A Banishment Spell

Let the twilight take it away
Let the sun set on your fragile bones
Let the blue-black rise with the moon
To swallow up
All of your own darkness
Give your darkness back
To the night
And may the stars of your heart
Be found again
Along with the
Rising of the moon
And on this black December night
May the bones in your flesh
Find rest
And be drained
Of all that pains you
There is no such thing as pain
There is no such thing as hurt
There is no such thing as being forgotten

Behind the Pink Rose

I have whispered a spell
From behind the pink rose petals
I have chewed on the rose
And drank of her nectar
By which I speak my
Enochian Tongue
A tongue of honey and milk
Spun on My lips
Concocted only for you
That I might have you
With me again
That I might know your
Warmth in my arms
Once again
That I may have your
Face buried
In my bosom
As close as the rose petals cling
To each other
So our souls shall
Hold onto
One another
Because I have whispered
An incantation
By the white candleflame
Like honey on my tongue
Were the hidden languages I
Chanted

C. JoyBell C.

To bring me back to you
From the nectar of the pink rose
Have come our longings
And our forever love
Poured into the night
Now the wolves
They howl for you
Now the moon
It is blue for you
My spoken words
Are soft and sweet
The tongue of angels
That guard at
Christ's feet

Fur

The only times she was forgotten
Were the times that she forgot herself
And forgot all the things
She truly longed to remember
The captured drops of memories
That evaporated too soon
Arose into the nostrils
Of her wolf
So even the things
She couldn't hold on to
He held onto them
For her
The scent of her
Stained onto
His fur
And the blood of her memories
Wrote themselves onto his eyes
How could she ever be forgotten?
When all of her and all that
Was left of her
Became one with the wolf

He Was Hers

It is a
very happy thing
to belong.

He thought he
never did belong
anywhere.

To anyone

Until the day
he found out that
he belonged to her.

I Never Knew

I never knew
that it would
be okay
That I would
be okay
I never knew this day
would come

Carry Me

If my feet grow too sore
And bloody from running
Would you let me climb onto your back?
I would bury my fingers
In your fur
Our breath would mingle
You'd take me away
I wouldn't need to run
Anymore
Because you
Would carry me

The Flea Market

I didn't really know what I was looking for
In that flea market long ago
I moved through the hoards of people
And for some reason, that day the afternoon
Glowed like heated amber
I moved through the crowds
Everyone thrice my height
I was little— that was a long time ago
I looked for something
There was something special there
Covered up in all that
Interesting old junk
It was somewhere… I could feel it…
There was a tall cowboy man
I remember him
And how he taught me how to
Know which watermelon to pick
He told me I had to knock on it
Three times with my knuckles
He made me laugh a lot
Because I like watermelons
But I kept on looking
Moving through the swarms of people
The air smelled like
Sweet cotton candy
And old men chewing on tobacco

C. JoyBell C.

It reminded me of the cheap fairs
I'd been to
Those places where I saw midgets
And real weirdness for the first time!
And places like the strawberry festivals
At night, after everyone had already
Gone home and the shortcakes cost only a penny!
After working my way down the rows of
Antique trinkets
I finally found what I was searching for!
It glistened under the amber sunlight
And when I picked it up I felt that
It had been warmed by
The afternoon summer heat
And by the hands before mine
That also held it
I smiled because I knew it was the one
I came there for!
A tiny pin barely visible underneath all those
Displays of eagle feathers
And peacock tails
A wolf pin
With emerald eyes
I asked my mother if I could keep it

The Lifting

In that place the winds were white and the white air
Left white streaks in my hair
While it lifted me and lifted my spirit
My skin and my soul
It was a place of serene solitude
The walls were washed in the white air, too
I think it's me stepping into the door of my heart
To see myself from the inside-out
Or maybe it's a place outside of me
Above me
That I am taken to, to remember things
To remember someone?
To remember you?
To remember me, too!
And all I can feel is a lifting
And all is gone away, passed away
All old things are passed away
The funny thing is that even as all old things
Pass away in that place
Somehow you have not
My wolf
But still, it is only me here, only all that is my own
Everything is empty, yet everything is full of me
So I am complete
Brought here by familiar voices
Accompanied here by familiar skin on my skin

C. JoyBell C.

There is one sofa
In the middle of this place
Where I sit to bathe in The Lifting
Outside is an unforgettable path
Strewn with transparent flowers
I always remember that path
It is always with me
Because I have the image of myself
Captured in my mind's eye
The image of me arriving
And I am loved
And I see myself
I see that I am loved
That I am fragile
But I am lifted, don't touch the ground…
I am home

Soul Mates

He has written her
Upon the iris of each his eyes
Into the specks of brown
Onto the streaks of grey
There you will find
Her threads of existence
The fabric of her essence
Sewn into his eyes

He has written her
Onto the tender,
Thin skin of his lips
Pressed into each line
Is the imprint of her mouth
The pattern of her palms
The embossment of the pores
On her thighs

He has written her
Into him
Until she has burst forth
Even into the texture of his hair
The color of his eyelashes
She grows out from beneath his skin
He carries her inside him
She can be found in his every pore

They are not two
But they are one

Not Sweet

I want to touch you
But not in the sweet ways
Not like holding your hand
Or stroking your face
There's nothing wrong
With the sweet ways
But that's not how I want to touch you
At least
Not right now

I want to touch you in the
Damn, maddening ways
That make my mind
Want to do flips
I want to touch you like
Hot coals
That burn bright
Orange-red
I want to touch you like
Grabbing onto life
Like you are
The skin of my skin of my skin
Of my soul and
My fingers and my thighs
And my breasts
Every part of me
That's how I want to touch you

In ways that
Make you bite your lip

C. JoyBell C.

Black Sheep

There is a sky above me
That softly rains
And a vodka bottle in my hands
Containing the stuff that comforts my soul
I am saturated in happiness
Down to the bone
Hair damp and messy
Just the way I like it
Skin strewn with raindrops
Just the way I like it
And in this very moment
Indian-sitting by a swimming pool
The smell of vodka and mango juice
Staining my lips
I am not good
I am a little bad
And I do not know where I belong
But I belong to myself
And this makes me happy

Like a Pretty Person

My wild, wild heart
Gets the best of me too often
In a way that
I'm not proud of
In a way
That I wish I could get rid of
Like an animal
Like an animal's heart
I just run away
In the ways
That only I know how to
And love?
My heart loves so wildly
The moment that it happens
They need to contain me
With bulls and with horses
Harnessed to my cage
A cage of ivory and iron
My heart—
It loves in all directions!
It can't become small enough
To be something pretty
Oh how I wish I
Could be less like an animal
More like a person
A pretty person
My brain explodes sometimes
When I love
I think it explodes
The other person's brain, too!

C. JoyBell C.

It's just not pretty
But it's real

I think I might be getting prettier
Now, though
After a couple of road kills

Lyrics

It's those songs that play on the radio
That kind of pull in the warmth
Of those forgotten and lost
Afternoons in the 80's
Those songs that melt
And tap into your olden memories
Those memories locked up that
Smell like Doctor Pepper spilled
Onto a steamy sidewalk in summertime
Skinned knees and water sprinklers
Watermelons and salted, cheesy potato chips
You sort of hate those songs
But then you can't stop singing them

They remind you of all that you didn't have
But then they remind you of all that you did
Have

C. JoyBell C.

My Black Lamb

I once had a black sheep
I was looking for a white one
But there were no white ones left
Not even a brown one or a spotted one
There was only a black one
The sun-dried lady held it up to me
Her toothless smile was
Blackened by tobacco stains
At first I was afraid
The Bible said that black sheep were bad
At least I think the Bible said that
Didn't the Bible say that?
I almost didn't buy the lamb
I almost didn't take him home
Out of fear
I was afraid of his blackness!
"I'll take him"
All I could look at were her
Blackened teeth, teeth à la noire!
As I said goodbye
The black lamb rode quietly in the van
With me, all the way home
My fear began to leave, fly away
Out through the van's window!
I smiled at the lamb
His eyes were dark as his wool
"You're my lamb," I cooed
I've been feeding him blackberries
For the past ten years

And they always ask me
Why and how could I ever
Take home a black lamb, not a white one!
"Are you being silly?"
I say to them
"His name is Caiden and he is
My very own lamb"
I suppose it's very silly
For anyone to be afraid
Of a lamb

Don't Forget Me, Please

The worst kinda hurt
Is being forgotten
By someone who
Is right in front of you
Watching the ways they
Knew you
Swiftly escape their eyes
Replaced with doubts
And fears
Because you said something
A little bit wrong
Because you acted in a way
They didn't understand
To be forgotten
While you are still there
To watch someone who
Truly knew you
Lose their faith in you
Begin to unknow you…
It hurts
I want to be forgiven
And believed in
I'm sorry for saying
Something wrong

These Scars

These scars on my face...
I'm hoping that they will show
The mountains that I climbed
When you look at these scars on my face
I hope that you will see
The odyssey
And not the brutality
If there be any brutality seen
May it be
The brutal, fierce will
Inside of me
I'm hoping that you won't look at me
And see a thing scarred
But I'm wishing that you will look at me
And see a thing that has won
A thing that is wild and has won
A thing that is still here
After all of that
And my scars to you must be
A map of survival
A digest to my heart
A proof of my existence here
All of that but not more
And none less

Covered

She grew long fangs
To protect her feather tongue
Sharp claws sprout from her fingertips
To surround cotton hands
The eyes that burn
Contain a soul that bleeds too easily
And the fur
The thick fur
Covers skin spun on cumulus clouds
Why must she cover herself
In order not to hurt?

Soil and Sky

I want us to gather
Lilacs together
Let's crush them between our fingers
The lilac flower juice
Will drip and color our palms
Trickle down our arms
Fall to the ground and
Seep into the soil

I want us to gather
Lavenders together
Let's crush them between our fingers
The lavender flower juice
Will drip and color our palms
Then we'll join arms
And fly into the skies
Where we will leave our lavender handprints

Let's stain the soil
And mark the skies

White Magic

Last night I was sad
So I stepped outside to cry
Took my slippers off
So the grass could
Make me feel better
I stood beside the
Indian Tree
Looked up into the
Dark sky
Tears rolled down
Sadness choked me
That's when I spotted
The three white bats
In the sky
They encircled
The patch of night above me
Round and around and around
They looked like big, white butterflies!
With their odd, bat-like patterns
They whisked to and fro
In circles
Above me
The white bats made me smile
They made me giggle
I stretched out my left hand to them
Like I wanted to reach them
And I wanted them to reach down to me
I wonder where they came from…

Humans Hurt

I'm afraid of them
She said to me
So I asked why
Because they hurt and burn and sting
They carry pitchforks
And thorns
If they see my eyes
And the softness of my skin
They will burn me
Cut me
And so I cover myself
With this cloak
She said to me
And I asked for how long now
Since I first found out
What they are like
Here, look at my scars!
They did this to me!
Now I hide under this emerald-colored hood
In these woods
Watch out
Humans hurt
She said to me
Then she also told me
That if only they hadn't
Harmed her

C. JoyBell C.

And left her with many scars
She would be just as she first was
So much more beautiful than now
And my heart cried to hear
These things that she said to me
First because of the tragedy
Second because it was true
And third because she couldn't see
That she was still beautiful
That she didn't need to hide

Your Every Hair

There are so many sufferings
In this world
Too many curses
Darkness
Scars and bleeding things
But when the gods look down
When the angels see us
Down here
They see beautiful things
Like the way every small curb
Of my body fits into the spaces of you
And how your fingertips
Skim the top of my backbone
While the sunlight
Through the trees
Makes outlines,
Patterns

On the rest of my skin
And your skin too

I think I can count your every hair

Voices and Stories

There is a voice
That's hidden between
The strands of her hair
The long locks that tumble
And crawl over her shoulders
There is a voice, a whisper
A gentle hum
And I can hear the voice
I can follow the whisper
I recognize the gentle hum
I can hum along
Voices overlapping
Like incantations
Made from the very fiber
Of the hair upon her head
And there is a touch, a vibration
That ripples and glides its way
From the surface of
The every crevice that her smile makes
On her face, from the
Every movement her muscles form
When she laughs, when she smiles
When she frowns
The shape of her lips imprint
A language upon
The very troposphere
Of all our beings
Every detail on her epidermis
Every line

Every pore
Every tiny hair
Has a song, hums a story
A song that is sung by
The otherworldly
A hum that is remembered
By those that are above

People

Just the way that people's flesh
Covers their bones
And creates a form
That's covered in that skin
Some freckled
Others dimpled
There are little hairs in all places
All of this together
Along with their sweat
The scent of pheromone
The specks of golden hew
In the eyes
Create etches
Against this stuff
We call the air around us
And sometimes they sigh
They close their eyes
Dust lands on their eyelashes
Sometimes
Or a snowflake when it's wintertime
And those eyes can contain
Fear or love
Sometimes fear and love at the same time
The way breath sounds on your ear
Is warm and hollow

But full at the same time
Full and held within itself
Within lungs and then upon lips
And nostrils
In and out
They breathe
In and out
And so these sketches move
And they feel and they seek
They are lost
And then found
They grow up and then down
All of these people

Unfold and Unfold and Unfold

They think they are just
Muscle and bone that is covered
In skin and hair and sweat
They think they can know each other
By looking at the way their feet point
To the door or to the window
They think they have known one another
By seeing how one leans in
And the other leans out
But what they really don't know is that
I can hear the way their hair hums
I can smell the scents that their eyes give off
Where their feet are pointed
Doesn't mean anything
The door is insignificant
The floor or the window don't matter
I can feel the weight of their soles
Pressing into the earth when they walk
Either a caress or a dispute
As if they walk upon my surface
Some kiss the ground with their feet
As they walk
Some stab the earth with their feet
As they walk
I hear the humming of the people

I know the scents of the humans
I read their songs— notes woven into
Their eyelashes
Stains left by tears of joy and
Tears of pain!
Those stains sing a song!
Each song unique
Each song one in seven billion!
They think they can read people?
Give me a telephone call
And I will recant to you the anthem
Of the demons in their voices
The anthem of the angels in their tones
Show me a person
I will unfold and unfold and unfold him

C. JoyBell C.

I, Angel

Why do people live their lives in a mold
 or in a pattern as defined by other people?
Why do children grow up learning to have visions
for themselves based upon what they see
on television and what their friends do and say?
Why do people hang their sense of fulfillment
Onto lines that have been drawn not by the hands of
ultimate truth— but by the hands of other mortals?
And the last question I have is this— why are humans loved
so much? There are so many things wrong with them,
and yet they manage to, in their simplicities,
captivate the heart of both God and Angel!
 In this sense, humans are dangerous. They are so loved and
yet because they do not know this, they always act as if
they're not loved, pulling both God and Angel into a
seemingly neverending struggle. In a way, I am tired of this.
Tired of everything. And yet I still admit that people are
captivating. What is it about their stupidity that makes you
want to guide them? What is it about their smiles that make
you want to smile back at them?

A Man in Love

There's something different that happens
To the air that's floating around
A man who is in love with a woman
There is a molecular change
A chemical reaction
I've observed this
It's the most captivating thing to watch
To feel, to see
I've seen it and whenever I see it
It catches me
I sit there (or stand there)
And watch how her every movement
Becomes the very magnetic pull
Of the blood in his body
Just as the moon pulls on the tides
Just like how the moon pulls on the oceans
Sometimes it's high tide
Other times it's low tide
But for a man in love with a woman
It's always high tide
I can feel that magnetic pull
Let's call it the lunar invocation
And everything has become
Only her
The way he breathes is made up of
Her happiness
And if you dare look at her
In a way he doesn't understand
Something ignites inside him!

C. JoyBell C.

He turns into her wolf
His very skeletal structure morphs
Nerves under his skin contract
And stretch out
Then contract again
The fire in his eyes says,
"What does that look mean?
Why do you look at her that way?"
Everything is about her
The oxygen that flows through his lungs
Wouldn't be worth having
Without her
Because his body would just
Lose its purpose
And the thing is
Usually she doesn't even know
Because she doesn't feel the lunar pull
She doesn't feel his nerves
Contract and extend
She can't see that the oxygen he now
Breathes is only the breath that she exhales!
She never knows
It's breathtaking
Time and time again I watch this
And it takes my breath away
The pull of her that is moon to him
Who has become her wolf
But the moon doesn't know the wolf
That howls at her in the midnight
Such is the case of
A man in love

See Me

I simply cannot see myself as one of them...
all the games that they play with each others' hearts and minds just go on and on and on...
they don't really love; they just happen to win. They don't ever find their other halves; they just find a thing and "make it work." They don't even know they have other halves to their souls! They don't even recognize the voice that calls in the winds. I'm just not one of them— they tire and bore me with their small, small lives that they think they have made so, so big with their reading of rules and tips and all their other sorts of shit.

They can say whatever stupid things they want to say; but I don't want to be a game someone wants to win; I want to be a person someone truly sees.

Three Hundred Years

I don't know what people talk about
When they talk about attraction
When they talk about
Chemistry
And then they go and make
Decisions of love
Based upon these laws?
These made-up laws and rules?

Because I imprint.
And I am imprinted upon.
My fingerprints embed into another's soul
And my own soul
Is clothed in a fingerprint
All over
It is imprinted
All over my soul

So I don't know what they talk about
When they talk about
Dating
And shit like that
I have three hundred years to live
And I will live it
Imprinted and imprinting

Come Away With Me

You have to be able to let go of
All the things you've learned and
All those things you thought you knew

And come away with me

Because all those tactics
And all those rules
Won't work on me

I am different

C. JoyBell C.

What You Want

So they tell you that another person
Will only value you
As much as you value yourself
And so
That means
If you value yourself this much
The other person will value you the same
But if you value yourself only this little
The other person will do the same

Fuck that

That's not what you want
What you want
Is someone
Who will look at all the
Dust and the grime and the mud
And the dung
Stuck all over you
And see the diamond on the inside
The diamond that is you

Creature of the Night

Creature of the night
Green aurora above the trees
Dark winds sway through the leaves
Bare feet
Sink into a patch of clovers

What We Are

It doesn't matter
What we're called
We are us

It doesn't matter what they
Think we are
Because we are us

I Did It

Who stole the moon?
It sat in solitude
Among the dark winds
Tonight
Just a minute ago
A little ways past
The aquamarine
Aurora Borealis
I see your footprints
In the clover patch
Right here
But no moon above

Where is the moon?

I was standing under
The Indian trees
Dark winds blanketed me
All over
Yes, those are my
Footprints
In the clover patch
Right there
Under the aquamarine
Aurora Borealis

True, there is no moon

I took the moon

Blackbirds

Blackbirds circle overhead
They sing a strange song
Fallen mangoes
Rot on the ground
They smell sweet
Do the blackbirds come for the
Rotting mangoes?
Or do they come to sing their song?

First rain of the year
Trickles onto my face
The drops skip when
They meet my skin

Closing my eyes,
I reach as high as I can
Into the sky with my hands
Underneath the mango tree
Beneath the blackbirds' orbit
And I smile

Right here, right now
I wouldn't want to be
Anyone, anyone else in the world
But me!

Flowers and Hearts

She pushed away every heart
That brought her love
And every hand
That gave her flowers
And I asked her why
"If I push them away
before they go away,
then that way I win"
she said.

And my heart bled
A drop of pure blood
To hear her story
First because she thought that
Love would always,
Always go away
Second because
It wasn't true but
She believed it to be true
And third because she thought
That she could win
This way

If only she could see
What it really means to win

To have the love in her heart and
To take the flowers into her hand

Peaches on the Ground

Here in the middle of the city
There is a funny rooster nearby
It makes me laugh to look at it
And I can smell a sea breeze
Almost taste the ocean's exhale
Though there is no sea anywhere around here
I suppose this smell and this taste
Has come from the Black Sea
So far, far away!
Standing here under this peach tree now
And on top of overripe peaches
That are rotting into the ground,
They are becoming a part of the soil,
Covering some stones in
Sickly-sweet over ripened goo;
I somehow feel as free as
The blackbirds above
They circle overhead
Are they here for the peaches?
Or are they here to sing to me?
Because I feel like they're here
Just to sing for me!
I feel happy, like
There are children running around
On top of my veins
And laughing louder and louder
Inside my arteries!
I have no visible reasons to be happy
Just like there are

C. JoyBell C.

No visible, rational reasons
Why I can smell and taste
The tide of the seas
From so very, very far away
And yet it is here
For no reason the sea breeze is here
And for no logical reason
I am happy
I'm not even wearing something nice!
There is a tear in the back of my pajamas
One that's been sewn
But you can still see where
It was torn! You can see the stitching!
There are so many practical reasons
For me to be unhappy
And yet I stand here
Under this peach tree
Atop these rotting peaches,
There are some flies
And I am smiling like
I am a quarter parts insane
I love it I love it I love it
Right here, right now
Nothing else, nothing else
I am happy

Wild

What does wild mean?
Does it mean running around
With a head that doesn't fit?
Does it mean
Losing sight
Of all that should not be lost?
Does it mean forgetting
Everything worth remembering?
Or does it just mean
Getting drunk
And dancing on tabletops?

No

Wild means
An unending peace
The look in your eyes
That spells forever
Wild means
Tranquility like a boulder
Immovable and everlasting
Wild means
The gentle smile
Is all it takes
To spin the world around

A small glistening in the eye

A Thought

Sometimes I have a thought
It is a thought of you thinking
That I might forget you,
That when you come back
I might not want you.

It makes me laugh a little.
I think it's funny, a little.
How could I ever begin to forget you
When I can feel you
Breathing inside my soul?
How could I ever begin
To unwant you
When I can feel your chest
Moving up and down
With every breath you take
Inside of me?

The Doe

If they had not torn it out of me
Away from me
The soft feathers
Of the cygnet
Would still be growing from
My fingertips
And
Had they not ripped it
From my chest
The heart of the doe
Would still beat within me

But I was torn
And I was
Ripped
So now I collect the feathers
Of the baby swan
I stick them back onto my
Fingertips
And I have
Received a new heart
The heart of a doe
She gave up her life
To restore my soul

I have lost
And I have found
Again

The Fawn

When you are
Gentle
Truly gentle
Life is difficult
And it's difficult because
Nobody else is gentle
Nobody else around
If there are others
They are far away
And far apart
Because this isn't
A gentle race
And it's not a gentle
Life
You will be a fawn
In a world of
Cheetahs
But I have come to learn
That beside every fawn
Stands a lion

C. JoyBell C.

Eat Cake and Laugh

You are too serious
You need to take your shoes off
More often
You need to laugh louder
And more than you laugh now
You need to eat weird things
And then laugh at the fact
That you eat weird things
Maybe one day
You should take off all your clothes
And jump into a lake
Maybe one day
You should walk around
In a patch of clovers
Barefoot
And watch the bats fly around overhead
While you try to take away the moon
Maybe one day you should
Turn into a wolf and say
"Oh how wonderful it is
To be so free like this"
And then you will eat cake
Lots and lots
Of cake
Drink some Vodka
Too

Better

I like animals better
They meet each other
They smell everything
All of their scents
Then they decide
If they like each other
Or not;
People meet each other
Put their best scent on
And like each other for that fragrance
Then when all the other scents
Come out
They run away!

I like animals better
They don't have a complex,
Advanced linguistic system
But they feel one another
On the inside
Because they feel
Exactly what it is
That they feel;
People have an advanced
System of communication
In different forms
Different writings

C. JoyBell C.

Various sounds
But they don't let themselves
Feel exactly
What they are feeling
They cover up so much
They are confusing!

I like animals better
Because when they're hungry
Or afraid
They will eat you
Or bite you;
People bite you
Even when they're not hungry
Even when they're not afraid
You never know
When they will bite you
And when they do?
They won't tell you the
Real reasons why!

I like animals

Wrapped in Purple Silk

Don't run away
From this darkness
Don't you know that it
Is wrapped in purple silk
Hidden away inside this heart
Tucked away where no one can see it?

Why do you despise this darkness?
It is the deepest treasure
Of this soul
Buried within a
Sigil-encrusted casket
Protected behind
Walls of thorny roses

Why do you run away
When you see the worst?
When it is the worst that is hidden
The worst is the treasure
Darkness is a treasure
It is kept and it is folded within
Covered within the beating and bleeding
Parts of the heart!

If you do not see the treasure
That this darkness is

How sad for you
To stand within a beating heart
And not recognize that you are inside it
And not know that
You feel the pain
You feel the fear
You feel the darkness
Because you are within
The most concealed part
Of the soul!

The best is not on the inside
The best is on the outside
It is the worst
That is on the inside
To feel one's worst
To openly see one's worst
Is to breathe within
A heart

Sapphire Blood

He wanted to make sure
That she was all she had said
She was
Or all the things she didn't say
She was
But that she acted like

So he thought

"There is no way to find out
If she is really the color blue
She might be black on the inside
Or green or yellow"

So he waited to see what
She would look like under the rain
And under the sun when it was naked
And under the snow when it was angry
And when she was stung by wasps
And when she was bitten by ants
So he sat and waited
He was so sure she would turn into
Black or green or yellow
But she didn't

C. JoyBell C.

So he thought, "Maybe if I tear a little at her petals
Then she will surely grow a thorn or two!"

But she didn't

And when he tore at her petals
They bled a blood that was blue!
Her petals were blue
And her blood was blue, too!
She was bluer than blue
Like a sapphire

Everything only made her more beautiful

Roses and Vanilla

I think that
The smell of your
Perfumed hair
Stays with me
Still
Unmoved by the winds
Unshattered by time
Roses and vanilla
Fragrance that still skips
In the puddles of my mind
Those places where
You used to be
With me
Splashing, laughing
Now I stand all alone
Here
With nothing but
Roses and vanilla

I miss you.

The Way We Are

I don't think that
You and I could
Ever be apart

I know it's been said
A thousand times before
Spoken by ten thousand tongues

Before us

But this time it's me
This time it's about
You and me

So it's special

You know?

We have to always
Stay together
Because that's just
The way we are

The Atheist

He fell in love
With her
In a way
That made him say
To himself
There must be a God

Just an Angel

Again and again
I am the price
The blood of the angel
That must drip to the ground
To soothe your soul

The others can love
And be happy
But when I love
There is redemption
A crown of thorns

I bear thorns in my flesh
To save you
Why?
Am I come into this world
From incantations?

Did I emerge
From a spell cast
Into the night winds
Over a bonfire
Beside the sea?

Have I no choice

To be happy?
Have I no choice
To love and be loved?
Just an angel

Is my blood not as worthy
As that of the human?
That my wounds
Are not tended to?
That people think it's okay

To forget me?

Medicine

You have to show me
Where your wounds are
Before I can
Bind your flesh
In healing oils

Freaks

We could dig up
Dry bones
From inside the caves
Uncover rubies from
The desert's cracks
Just to show you
Just to make you feel
How we know things
How we see and feel things
We could call on angels
Higher powers
Just to make you see
What we are
Maybe the Kings
Or the Cherubs
Can tell you
How we were made
By what tongue
We were pronounced living
Breathing and moving
Because you wonder how we
Read your thoughts and
You wonder how we
See so much and
You think we might be
Freaks

Don't burn us
At the stake

Quiet My Demons

I love you in a way
That makes me believe in things
Like gods, angels and demons

That kind of love

The way your skin feels
On top of mine
To me are both god and angel

The way you quiet my demons
Makes me see
All the things wrong with me

That you whisper away

Raspberries and Leather

I am sensuous
I am things that are
Deep and smoldering
Scarlets and suedes
Raspberries and leather
Vanilla and the humid air

I am sensuous
Don't place me in a polished box
My scent would break through it
Anyway

Before and After

It lingered in all those years
Before I met you
The happy spaces
That weren't happy enough
Just because I
Didn't have you yet

Here
In my arms

And then it began
In a new way
In a reinvented way
Happy spaces that
Were finally happy enough
And even better than enough!

Because you came along
And filled my arms with you

The Smell of the Air

There is
The sound of wind chimes
A truck coming up
That dirt road
And the smell of
Wildflowers, grass and smoke.

Everything

Familiar as always

But the way that you're
Not here
Is an open wound
In everything I know
In everything that's familiar
So everything that should comfort

Me

Cannot comfort me

Because in your absence
You have torn away at it all
And nothing that's left
Is worth anything without you
Even the way the chimes sound
Even the smell of the air

He Whispered To Me

"You have become my soul
Inside of me
From inside of me
I can feel a heartbeat
That's not mine
And I don't think
That's possible
Or that it's ever possible
To happen
Every day
Over and over again
How deeply can one fall in love?
Does it never stop?
When I looked into the other women's eyes
The ones before you
I didn't even know that
This kind of thing existed
So you're a fool to
Be afraid
A fool to be insecure
When my own soul has
Been eaten by my bones
And all that's left in between my skeleton
Is you
All that's contained within my skin
Are my flesh, bones and your soul

I feel your heart beat
Where my heart is supposed to be
I feel my blood ooze from my body
Just to make space for you
On the inside"

Our Kind of Love

There are so many kinds of love
And you can always write about them
You can always write poems
And stories, novels and prose

Then there's our kind of love
It's the kind that
You don't want to write about
Because you wanna keep everything to yourself

every

last

drop

of

it

ssssssssshhhhhhhh…

How You Found Me

It's probably the only reason
Why we came back
Here
To find each other again
I guess I fell down first
You followed after searching Venus
And Jupiter
The Moon and Mercury
All the stars in Pleiades
When you couldn't find me there
You came here

All my life I have needed you

Far

There is this wretched
wretched stupidity called

being
so
far
away
from
you.

That Nightmare

It's a thick, dark thing that blinds
Pulling me downwards in my dream
Into a place
Where I kneel and beg for love
Onto a floor that knows
The shape of my knees too well
I beg not to be left
I plead for love
It's always a familiar face
That looks down at me
There
At the feet of the people
I love most
I find myself
Sometimes
In that same dream
It is
Ripping and ripping
At the skin of my soul
Tearing and tearing
At the fabric of my subconscious
There's nothing I want more
Than to get out of the nightmare

When I wake up
I'm left with the gnawing

C. JoyBell C.

Aching of it
I wonder
If the gnawing aching
That sticks to me
Is sometimes why
I push people away
All those faces who stood above me
In the nighttime haunting
Maybe some part of me fears
It wasn't just a dream

Stealer of Souls

The sunlight today was beautiful
While it set
Behind the rainclouds
And smog
It felt like songs
Escaping from anguished lips
It felt like
Hymns
Setting themselves free
From parched, cracked lips
And there was something
Beautiful about that

It took me away
It stole my soul
The sun stole my soul

Fright

My greatest fear
Is asking someone to
Stay
I don't want to
Ever, *ever*
Ask anyone not to leave

Today I thought
How long will I be afraid?

One day
When I tell someone that
He's not allowed to leave
That day will be
The most frightening day

Spaces in Between Us

There are moments of silence
Spaces of quiet that
Stretch
In between us

Not to worry

They are the times
During our dance
That we step back

To look at the
Beautiful thing
We've created

Together

This beautiful thing
Called us

Stay

I can get pricked
Too much
Sometimes
If a thorn goes deep enough
It can push me back
Into somewhere
Where I begin to forget
Things begin to fade
I begin to renew myself
But sometimes I want it to stop
So I can remember
Because there's not just bad
There's good too
But the pain
The prick
It forces me to forget
Everything
And I stop believing

The only one who
Can make me remember again
Is the one in my dreams at night
So I look for him
Over and over again
I look for him

I want him to *say my name*
And never
Ever leave me

Vampire

I wish that I could
Reach into your chest
With my own fingers
And wrap my hand
Around your heart
Feel it beating
Against my palm
That way
I would *feel* you
All the way down to
The beating of your heart
Against my own hand
My fingers would move
Up and down
While it beats
And I would look into your eyes
To see how you look at me
When your own heart
Knows the warmth of my hand
For the first time

But I would have to be
A vampire
To do that!
And you would have to be one
Too!

Or you could be a werewolf
And I would love you
All the way down
To your beating heart
And that look in your eyes

So I guess
I will just have to become
A vampire
And you will have
To become
Something
Too

Again, Please

It was like something
That I had been waiting for
My whole life
To hear

It was like something
I was waiting my whole life
To drink of
I thirsted for it

You were the breath
Dangling at the tip of my tongue
And I had to inhale you
With another word

One more word
One more conversation
Again, please
Can I hear your voice again, please?

I want to ring you back

More

I want to be
More
Than just your girlfriend

I want to be
Your home

I want to be your family
And you to be mine

I want us to belong to each other

You belong to me
And I belong to you

C. JoyBell C.

Light a Fire

I will light a
Fire for you
Though not in the burning
Maddening ways
But I will light
A flame for you
Just one
For you and
All you do

You and I
Forever

The Prayer of Fire

There is a place
In a time of old
When one's dress
Was olden
Forgotten
You can go to that place
When you're given the scroll
With words written
In flames
Erupting
At the slightest glance
When your eyes scan the paper
There is a message only you can read
Written by the finger
Of fire
Written by your heart's desire
From century upon century
Lit for the one
Whom your heart
Yearns for
And you take the scroll
To the tomb of stone
In that meadow

While I walked into the meadow
By the trees
In the long-forgotten dress
I felt remembered
And recognized
Though I did not remember

C. JoyBell C.

And though I did not recognize

There stood the tombstone
Where many left their prayers afire
I too, stood there with my paper
I almost put it in the grave
But then
I thought of you
You are not dead
You are just outside
Of that place of meadow and tree
You are there, you are here
The blazing prayer should stay with me
And I will ignite your skin
And mine
While this incantation of passion
This centuries-old prayer of passion
Consumes us

I almost left the burning paper on
The tombstone
As the written fires
Turned into small yellow roses
But I remembered you are not beyond
In death
Only beyond the dream
Here in this realm
I shouldn't call you from
Beyond the grave
You are here now
You are already mine

Darling

They attempt to speak of what I am
Of where I'm from
What I'm made of
How many names
Do they have for me?
By many different tongues
They call to me in the mornings
Or in the evenings
Some have no name at all
Some don't see
Don't feel and don't hear
At all
And you think I have forgotten you
But I have not
Darling,
You have forgotten yourself
And the patterns of your dance
The rhythm that your heart makes
When your head lies upon
My chest
Forgotten
But I have not forgotten you,
Love
Lay your head upon my shoulder
And I will remind you
Of you

C. JoyBell C.

Take These Lilies

There is a place
Where the Blood of the
Son of God
Dripped to the ground
On top of a hill
Lily of the Valley
Sprouted
A white blossom
For every drop of Blood
That fell
And if you gather this flower
Bind it upon your wrist
You have gathered and bound to you
The Freedom
Shed by the Flesh of the Son
You are freed from The Accuser
In this life
In all your past lives
And all the ones to come
A return of happiness
Where happiness was once gone
Brought back by the Work of the
Son of God
Take these Lilies
Bind them around your neck
The vipers they see it
The serpents they know it

You need not fear, anymore

A Very Sad Story

He tested her and tested her
Until her hands were raw and numb
It was very sad; he didn't see how long she had
Waited and waited
For him, didn't hear how many times she
Called out his name into the fire
Hoping he would find her
So when he did, by that time
All that was left was her skeleton
Transparent and weightless
Bones with a small life still left
Cracked in many places
So when he tested her many times
The bones became dust, ashes in the sunlight
She never got to know that he, too
Had remembered her. He was just too scared.

Belong

You will only belong
To the one who
Sees your worth
Because you are a rose
And you must belong
To the one who will pay for
The price of a rose
Not a daisy
Not a weed
Not even a tulip!
But a rose. The price of a rose.

You will only belong
To the one who
Sees your worth
Because you are a sapphire
And you must belong
To the one who will pay for
The price of a sapphire
Not an opal
Not a turquoise
Not even a pearl
But a sapphire. The price of a sapphire.

Why?

I wished to cover you in roses
To heal your every wound
But you kept on
Stabbing your skin with
Old thorns
Ones that aren't even
There anymore
You couldn't see me
Placing my rose petals
On top of your
Bleeding veins
You couldn't see me
You couldn't see me

The Foreigner

They say I am different
But I would have to disagree
I am different here, yes
But there is a place where I
Am like all else around me
A place where the air
Matches the tincture in my eyes
I remember my home
Hectares and hectares
Of yellow tulips
Growing taller than me
Where peace
Leaks out of every cell
That makes up my bones
And tissue and muscle
My home is within me
Even while I am here with you
That's why you think I'm different
Because these runes make sense to me
Because these sigils match my DNA
Because my presence is different
Than yours
I'm not like you
But I'm not really different
I'm just not from around here

"Blame and praise have no true effects. Is an emerald less lovely, if it is not praised? Or is gold less lovely, or ivory, or the color purple?... I am committed to be an emerald, and keep the colour that is mine."

~ Marcus Aurelius

Keep The Colour

It is not for you that I
Am the perfection of emerald

It is not because of your
Absence or presence
That my purple blood does not fade

It is nothing owed to you
Or planted against you
That my sapphire heart
Beats warm like gold

I look not to the world
For solace nor for a scapegoat
To explain the colours or the fadings
Of me
But

It is unto mine own spirit
That I am true

C. JoyBell C.

It is unto mine own nature
That I stand immoveable
It is unto mine own soul
That I must and will be genuine
I am sapphire
And I will keep the colour that is mine

Hey, You!

I am so tired of running away from
myself and all of
my broken pieces
that I
cut my feet on.

But

If someone were to stay,
then I would stay with me, too.

Hey, you!
Stay with me!

What Are We?

What is it that we are?
How can our hearts beat together
Skip together in a single unison
When we are two different people?

What are we?
That I can look into your eyes
And see your soul from
A hundred and one miles away?

What is it that we are?
You can see my memories
You can roam in my dreams at night
And you are a hundred and one miles away?

What are we?
That time and space know
Us not?
We are above them both!

What is this, what are we?
What are we?
That a hundred thousand years
Can all become a minute

A single minute
Shared between you and I
Just a thought
Is all it takes

Just a memory, just a mingling
A mingling of our pieces
Pieces that break off of us
And fly into each others' eyes

Cutting deeply into each of our souls
What are we?
What is this?
Where are we from?

Film Noir

In my dream last night
It was all black and white
For the first time
Because I usually never dream
In black and white
But last night I was in Rome
Back where my soul longs to be
And I met a woman
Who owned a small school
Of business
Who liked to dance in the rain very often
I remember every detail of her face
And how her hair was
Not perfect
But was messy
A bit
And so I wondered if that was me
In another life, long ago
In black and white
And she said to me
"In this life you either
Learn, or do, or die trying."
Then I watched her run off into the rain
On the cobblestone streets
Of Roma
I've just awoke now

My eyes are still heavy
And aching
But I had to write this down
Lest I forget her words of wisdom
The words of wisdom from the black and white
Woman in my dream last night
Who could have been me
In another life

No Longer Alone

They speak the tongues of the Angels
And gather together
At the place where
The moonlight escapes
The shadowy sun
Ancient tunes be on their lips
Their skin combusted
By the mere presence
Of one another
This is where
And how
Their existence confirms
It's reality
But what they are
Or what names are given to them
Is something of mystery
Unknown, enshrouded
They seek to find
The answers to whom they are
What they are
But for now
To converse in the tongue of
Gabriel and Michael
Is the very essence
Of them
And I will leap!

Leap forward because
I am now no longer alone

Drink This

Break the ruby
Crush the emerald
Pour out the sapphire's heart
Into this golden chalice
Marked with the tongue of Malachim
And let the people drink
So that they might know
The secrets
The protected treasures
Of old
Of beyond and before
Of now and then and always
Of the brothers and the sisters
Of The Ineffable One

Hidden Cherub

Suburban New York
Happens to conceal
Her wings well

Draped in shadows
Of concrete buildings
Nobody else can see them

Eyeliner always too dark
And thick
Hiding her pretty face

Or does she
Really want to hide
From herself?

From who she is

Because it's hard to
Have huge wings
Growing out of your back

When no one else can see them

Wings

She dreamt of him
Always

He dreamt of her too
Always

Every night

And they didn't know
If the other even existed

For real

But they
Recognized

Each other
In deep sleep

They were always together

They saw
Each others' wings

Coordinates

From the very first day
I read your name out loud
And felt the sound of it
Roll off my lips and tongue
I knew you
And I remember the coordinates
Of you and I
42.4300° N, 18.7700° E
That's where we first made love
That's a place I haven't even been to
But I remember it
Those numbers are
Carved into my arteries
Because my memories of you
Are things I find in my dreams
At night
They're more than just dreams
They're how my mind remembers us
Remembers longitudes
And latitudes
That I don't even recognize
So I know the coordinates of us
From a place I've never even been to
Even if I wanted to escape you
I couldn't
We are bound together

Lycanthropy

He said to me
"You make me feel animalistic
Like I want to eat meat
The whole day
Like I have fangs
And am covered in fur
You turn me into an animal"
And I told him
That he turns me into an animal
Too
He asked me if that didn't frighten me
"Why aren't you afraid of that?"
So I said to him
"It sounds to me like
I turn you into a wolf
And you turn me into one, too
Or maybe it's just me who's turning you
Into something like me
Why would I be afraid of that?"
The look in his eyes said
Because an animal is an animal
That's why
So I asked him
If he didn't know that
Wolves are bound to only one other
Unlike the humans
Wolves love only one
Forever

Demi-god

As your body was conceived
Being formed in the womb
Human
Your soul came in
From a place
Not human
And this is what it means
To be half god
How funny of them to think
That it means your mother is human
And your father is a god
Or that your father is human
And your mother is a goddess
But I forgive them for they can
Only ever see through their human eyes
But we know differently
To be half god
Means that your body is human
While your soul is not.
One half human
The other half a goddess
Both a hundred percent their nature
One inside the other
You do, in fact
Equal two hundred percent

C. JoyBell C.

Enochian Prayers

I think I listened long enough
And hard enough
Through the crack in that door
I found the spell
To call to you
So I could hear your voice

I think I listened long enough
And hard enough
Every day through that crack
In their door
As they spoke of things like
Salamanders and sylphs
Eagles and antlers

And maybe the incense I inhaled
Was too much
Or just enough
To awaken the Enochian prayers
In my fingertips
And on my tongue

Because one night I spoke
The tongue of the Angels

And then I heard your voice
You called to me
In the midnight hour
You spoke to me
Your voice walked through me

As if I were nothing but a ghost

C. JoyBell C.

Comedere Rosae

I have nine long-stemmed
Pink roses

I have nine long-stemmed
White roses

I have nine long-stemmed
Yellow and red roses

I have a pair of scissors
I will cut off the flowers
Put them into wooden bowls
The thorns and the leaves
Go into the trash
But the stems I will shred
Like carrots

Then I will set the table
With the finest of china
And we will eat these roses

There will be a dash of cinnamon, too

Weird

I remember the midget sitting on the tiny chair
In a trailer car parked at the side of the fair
A small, black woman
Who wouldn't smile at me
She refused to smile at me
I think
And in her eyes
I could see that she thought I was weird
And that was strange
Since *she* was the little person
The tiny person
That we were paying money
Just to look at
She never smiled
Not even for a moment
She looked at me and I thought she might
Be thinking, "What is this little
Half-Asian child doing here?"
So that made me feel
Like maybe I should have a little chair
Sit right beside her
Maybe people would pay money to see
A little multi-racial child
Like me

Weird (2)

That afternoon we all went out
To spend time together at the mall
Shopping, lunch and a movie
Baltimore, Maryland
I remember my cousin Amy
Picking out new skirts with my mother
And my auntie
Everyone was blonde
They all had blue or green eyes
My eyes and hair were dark
So different from everyone else's
And siting in the movie house
The boys in front turned around
To ask Amy a question
About the popcorn, or something
The boys were cute
And had blonde hair too
I could see their hair glowing like glow sticks
In the dark
That's how blonde they were
And I was glad the lights were off
That we were in a movie house
Because that way
Maybe the boys would think I
Looked just like them
Or that I looked just like Amy
They couldn't see I was
Multi-racial

With hair too dark and eyes too deep
But that was a long, long time ago
I was just a girl
Only eight

I felt like I was weird

She, The Moon

Her face was poke-marked
Like the Moon
You don't look at the moon
Covered in all of her comet-scars
And think, "Oh she's so ugly!"
No, it's never like that, really
You look up at the moon and you see the
Places where comets hurt her
The evidence of where asteroids hit her hard
And you say, "She's so, so, so beautiful!"
And you say, "I wonder what each crater means
I wonder where each one came from!
How I would like to know!"
So then you start studying Astronomy
Just because of beautiful scars
And that's how I felt when I saw her face
It glowed from within, just like the Moon
It wasn't smooth, just like the Moon
And her eyes, just like the moon
Made me ask what happened to her
I wanted to wonder and to wonder
About her story
I wanted her to tell me
All of her stories
Where each and every crater in her heart
Came from
And why there were marks on her face
And then I wanted her to explain to me
Exactly why

She doesn't think that she's beautiful
If the Moon didn't think she was beautiful
I would think the Moon was being ridiculous
And then I would ask her, "Why don't you think
You are beautiful?
Because you are!
Sometimes, you're even more beautiful
Than the Sun!
And you glow and swell in
The night
Like the night's not even there!"
I would say that to the Moon
I would!
So can I say that to you now?
Why don't you think you are beautiful?
Because you are!
You're just like the Moon!

Uncovered Pizzas

I was never carried away into
Exaggerated joy
Or flights of fantasy
When visiting the circus
Or when visiting the fair
Surrounded by caramel-coated apples
And the smell of salty popcorn
I was never as elated as
All the others around me
I would look into the heat of the day
And wonder why I didn't have enough
In life
After the circus was over
And we'd go home
I knew I'd go home to less
Than what other people had
And it wasn't okay
The heat of the day
And the little goldfish
Swimming in plastic bags
Wouldn't be permanent
I knew
So they passed by my eyes
Temporal, passing things
Fading Christmas lights
Tied around food huts

Flies landed on the uncovered pizzas
Thinking about so much
At such a young age
Always wanting to be far away
Always wanting something more

C. JoyBell C.

Chopsuey

My life
For too long now
Has been a series of
Getting food poisoning
From stuff like chopsuey
And damn hotdogs on sticks
Feeling incredibly happy
Over the smallest of things
Taking naps and
Waking up to the very same routine
All over again
I'm tired of finding joy in the
Simplest of things
I'm tired of
Getting food poisoning
From chopsuey
I'm tired of waking up
Under the same roof
On this same bed
There's this hum in my head
A broken record playing in my brain
I'm tired of all this
Character building
Or molding
Whatever it's called

I'm through with this
Where's my plane ticket?

American Indian

She stood there and asked me
Where are you from?
Her face hovered above mine
And she had the sweetest intentions
Didn't mean anything bad at all
But I choked a little
On the mere motions my mind performed
While it frantically looked inside
The boxes in my brain and behind
The curtains and under the carpets
For an answer
To that simple question
Where was I from, anyway?
I don't think I really knew
Where are you from, sweetheart?
I'm from here, I'm American
I answered
Are you American Indian?
Her smile was big and
Was beginning to look ignorant
I am a little, but not so much, I said to her
And then I didn't even want to
Talk to her anymore
I was so sorry that I felt that way
And angry why it was so hard for me
To answer a simple question

Filippa, Filippa!

Filippa, Filippa!
Why don't you reach out
To touch the roses
Anymore?
My own reflection beckoned
To me in the mirror
The surface of that glass
Vibrated, like a rippled lake
I am just too different
I whispered back to myself
I looked down at the rose
Drawn, almost sewn
Deeply into my skin
The palm of my hand
Reminding me of childhood
Trips to McDonald's
My own laughter in my ear
Filippa, Filippa!
Remember the song in the wind!
My windows were closed
I had forgotten to believe
I opened my window
And let in the windsong
His song
It became the air
In my lungs
Filippa, Filippa!
He soon comes!

Filippa, Filippa! (2)

Filippa, Filippa!
Why is your eye kohl too thick
And dark?
It hides your beautiful eyes!
I watched her grow
From a girl who spoke of
Constellations and windsongs
To this woman who
Has forgotten the colour
Of her own eyes
I asked her if she remembers
The boy just like her
And she said she hadn't seen him
In a while
She hadn't seen Andromeda
In a while, either
I think that made her sad
More sad than she
Should ever be
So there she sat by the river
Or under the Holly Tree
Where she forgot things
And remembered things
Filippa, Filippa!
I think I see him
I think I hear him howling
At the sun
Riding on the moonshine
Running in the winds
He soon comes!

C. JoyBell C.

Ezekiel

He was perched high up in the sycamore tree
Like a soulless bird, perched up on a branch
The autumn winds picked up the yellow-orange leaves
That had strewn themselves on the path
Through the thicket
The way his eyes looked into mine
Made me feel like he saw behind
My walls
And all the faces I had put on
Just to get through that one day
All the things I needed to show the world
Were worn one on top of the other
But he saw the real me
The me that was me that was just me
But then he saw more
He saw my secrets, too
How and why?
"Who are you!"
I called up at him
The wind blew suddenly and harshly,
Casting goosebumps across my arms
And onto the back of my neck
"Why are you watching me!"
He didn't say a word but
I knew his answers,
I could hear his voice in my heart
Answering me
"I am Ezekiel
And I know you well

I know your secrets
I know how you grow roses
From your palms
I know how you speak
voces magicae
I know how you
Brought that dead bird
Back to life
A long time ago…"
His eyes looked soulless
But not in a bad way
Only in a way that made me think
That maybe there are other
Kinds of souls
Not just one kind of soul
Not just human
And what's more is
He felt like home!
"How do you know that!"
My voice trembled a little, I think.
"How do you know that about me
And why are you up there in that tree!
Why are you watching me?
Are you psycho or something!"
But then I felt the sting
Of my own words
They stung my tongue as I spoke them
"I'm sorry"
I whispered in my mind
And then he answered
"I have been with you always
I know your secrets
Because they are my secrets, too"

C. JoyBell C.

Text Messages

Zeke?

> Yes.
> That's my name! ☺

I wanted to ask you something.

> Okay, but hurry I have to run out in a minute.

Did I find you? Or did you find me?

> I think you found me. ☺

I did? ☺

> Yes. Well, what do you mean?

I wonder if I found you or if you found me.
I wonder about if it was you or if it was me.
Sometimes I think you found me.

> Maybe we found each other.

Backdoors

The ways that I let you in
Are different
The doors are different
When I meet someone and I decide to
Let them in
I know exactly
Which doors to open
Which walls to lead them to
So they can break down those same walls
With their sledgehammers

But with you it's different
It's so, so different
You know where my backdoors are
So you come in that way
You go to the backdoors, open them
And suddenly you're inside!
You don't even need to tear
Any walls down
In fact
You say that it's okay to have walls
And that you don't want to break them down
You say that in the way you talk to me
I know that's what you mean
Well now I know why

Because you remember where my backdoors are
I don't even remember
But you do

Eagle Chief

The Chief wore eagle feathers on his head
And he was just standing there
Looking at me
The way he looked at me was different
It was like he was seeing something
Which nobody else saw
I was scared
His eyes were like daggers
Did I do something wrong?
Had I wandered onto sacred burial grounds?
Was he going to curse me?
He never stopped watching me
Looking at me
The strength of the sun
Shone from his face
The vision of the very same bird
Whose feathers he wore on his head
Shared with him its vision, too
They were one
The eagle and the chief
What did he see in me?
I really didn't know
I thought I had done something wrong
But now
The eagle comes to me in my dreams
With a wingspan encompassing
All power, all might, all grace
And it sits on my shoulder

Its talons grip my shoulder
And our vision is one
We are not two
We are just one
Its wingspan
Is my own wingspan
All that it has
It has given to me
I remember the Chief
The way he looked at me
The way he never stopped looking
At me
And I realize, I think
That maybe I hadn't done
Anything wrong, at all

But I still wonder
What he saw in me

Murr-Ma

(v.) To walk around in the water, searching for something with your feet.

It's not even funny
How she thinks she came from the waters
And I think so, too
I think she came from a mixture
Of soft turquoise sea foam
And indigo scoops from where
The sea is at her deepest
It would be a foamy froth
With a very deep heart of indigo
Violet
Like the oceans when they roll
And crash
In her dreams at night

What does it mean?
To be born of the waters?
Does it mean that she is colorful?
Does it mean that she is different?
Or are we all born of the seas?
Are all of our souls watery?

Maybe it means she fell off of a ship?
Or was conceived of the loins of Poseidon?

But then sometimes her eyes ignite with fire
So what is it, really?
What is the answer to that song
Which her spirit sings
In the form of a
Long riddle
Difficult to grasp
Far away and yet
Right there in her heart

Breathe

At once
The waves overcame me
As you know they would always do
And that's why you toss me
Into your seas
You like to see me turn
And turn
Like a sea serpent
In the waves that
Lick
At my skin
But your whisper
In my ear
"I will take you
To my bed"
Calmed the roaring waves
Melted off the foaming salts
That tickled my pores
I was with you
In your bed
Sea-drenched
Ocean-soaked
Tangled in moonlight
The bursts of your whisper
Inside me
Ignited

My own internal moon
And I shone
For you
I glowed
For you
In your bed
Taken in by a whisper
Forever and a day
Within a moment.
And I would be safe
Here in your bed
Safe from all the things
I protect myself from
I would be safe
For every day of my life
If I share a bed with you
Now the tingling salts
The lapping waves
Are down below the cliff
Where we can hear them
From a distance
But the sound of your breath
Is home

C. JoyBell C.

Purple Silk

We always calculate
How much we give
Because we are so afraid
Of giving more
Than what we can receive
From the other
And so our love becomes
A dance of back and forth
Back and forth
Fear and trust
Doubt and hope
But if only you could
Stand
In the you
Of the you
That is you
That is you
That is you
Like purple silk
Breaking out from
A crusty mold
You would unfold
Over and over again
Over and over again
Over and over again
Into yourself and
Into and into
And into
Then

You would be so strong
It wouldn't matter what
The other could give
Or couldn't give
It wouldn't matter what
You could get
It would just be
A beautiful thing
Immeasurable
Indescribable
Like the way love was
Made to be

C. JoyBell C.

With This Pen

I will take a paper
And with my pen
Write upon it
The virtue of you
That runs through my veins
I will write you
Into every line of my
Past
Present
Future
You will find yourself
In the white spaces
Between
Each chapter
Each paragraph
Every sentence
Every word
Even in the tiny white spaces
Between each letter
And the white spaces
In and around every letter's form
There you will find yourself
You will recognize your own skin
Folded and folded into the
DNA of my penmanship
And I will give you breath there
Therein you will
Breathe

The breath that I have breathed
Through time
All this time
And all of it to come
You will let go of your own breath
To share in mine
And my pen will write your flesh
Into my flesh
And the two of us
Will be one

Don't Cry

She threw herself open for him
Both her heart and her body
Because she was angry
And she thought that
It would be what every man
Wanted
But he didn't want that
He didn't want her body
Nor her heart
And that broke her
In the City of Paris
And she fell in love with
Another man
Gave him her vulnerability
Let him see how much
She wanted to stay with him
To be with him
But he just left
Because he didn't want
Her and her vulnerability
He didn't want to give up
His racy life of light, alcohol
And dancing
In the City of Buenos Aires
She gave everything to
Yet another man
Her whole trust
She told him she wanted him
To keep her

But he went away, too
He promised he would always
Stay
He promised he
Would never leave her
He said, "Please keep me, too"
But he never called again
In the City of Casablanca
Yet another man
Stole her heart
They dreamed together
They planned together
But he couldn't get away
From his demons
And he told her
His demons were her fault
She had to leave him
Because he hurt
Too much
She had to say goodbye
To promises and dreams
They built together
In the City of Santa Fe
I found her one day
On her bed, in the darkness
Of her room
There alone, it was humid
In the City of Seville
"Why do you cry?"
I stroked her hair
I whispered to her,
I showed her my face and said,
"They're not the one.
Don't cry. He soon comes."

C. JoyBell C.

Vodka

Last night I discovered
That I like myself
A whole lot better
When I have alcohol in my blood
Preferably Vodka

Touch

I feel different today
You know?
I feel like I could tell you
A thousand and ten things
But those things wouldn't
Compare to touching you
To knowing what that feels like
What your skin feels like
So these things that I could say
All a thousand and ten of them
Have become the smile
On the corner of my lips
And a desire to poke you
With the tip of my finger
Poking you would make me laugh
You know that, right?
But more than that I want to hold
Your hand and touch your face
Aaaawww gosh
This is just too sweet
My words are too sweet
I should make this into a poem
Or something
But really though
Today is that day
It's the holding hand day
Do you like to do that?
Because when I get to be with you
I will be holding your hand

A Heart

So I was looking at this photograph
that I took while in Florence.

A cordiform

Fuchsia flower petals blown in the wind
were stuck onto the water in a puddle.

Along with some trash

It was a perfectly-shaped heart
right there on the ground.

Piazzale Michelangelo

So I thought to myself
while I looked at this photograph I'd taken

"Now isn't this what real hearts
are made up of?"

Flower petals and a bit of trash

Effluvia

Tonight is different
I can't write anything down
I can't say anything
I can hardly think

The moment I pick up my pen
The things in my heart dissipate into
Molecules of fragrance
The smell of honey
And passion fruits

The minute I open my mouth
The concealed words escape my tongue
Running off of the edge
Like wild horses jumping a cliff

I can hardly even think
The very second I begin to
Form a thought
Effluvia.
Effluvia happens

I don't know what's happening to me
I think I might be turning into
Air
Or maybe water

Into something else
Definitely

C. JoyBell C.

Lullaby

I'm sure there are many out there
Who would want to take their
Happiness away from them
Because theirs is a happiness
Beyond understanding
With no tangible reasons of existence
Their happiness is AEther
Eternal like a fifth element
Provided by hands of gods
These hands crawl over cloud and mountain
These hands crawl over rock and
Grain of sand
To creep into their hearts
And nail the happiness inside of them
Where nobody can take it away!
So they are different in that
They need no one
They may have once wanted
To need, to be accepted and remembered
But now they have grown
Into their own skin
And the people wonder why
They are so happy, they can be so happy
The mundanes wonder
How they transmutate
All fear, all hate, all envy
These two whom were once
Beaten and stoned
Bowed down low
They now laugh as if

They have known no pain, no injury
They're cradled in
The arms of gods

Jacob's Ladder

How am I supposed to know
Where to go
When I am half of this
And half of that
A beacon of that world
An illumination in this one
I remember
When we cascaded down the
Tall fleet of stairs
The first time
Life was spoken
Into our marble bodies
And veins began to grow
Blood began to flow
We moved down the long flight of stairs
Leaping and perching
From step to step
We moved like leopards
As our lungs sprouted and grew
From our backs
The very first time we knew the taste of breath
I remember that day
And how it felt
When color started to fill our irises
Like drops of viscous dye in water
I saw how the color came upon

The eyes of my brothers
As we cascaded down
The stairs
Into this world
Into this realm
Down below
And here I am now
I sit
On this subway train
Eating a corn dog
While blue blood
Pulses through these veins
And a heart
Beats in my chest

Jacob's Ladder (2)

Why do I let open my door
And allow my window
To hang on its hinge
Creaking in the dark winds of midnight
Why do I wait
So tirelessly for you?
Why do I stand here in this door?
Only a candle in hand
To light this hallway
I hope to see your shadow
Cast on the walls
My memories are roamed
By your presence
I feel you when you look at me
Like the olden days
Of beyond
From before the descent
I can feel your shadow cast upon my skin
Even your shadow bears weight
Upon my flesh
You are the footprints on my body
I remember you from the olden ways
You were my guardian
Your presence always near
The vampires always nigh
Could not harm me

Could not hurt me
Could not take my soul from me
Not any part of it
For you stood before me
And I behind you
Many a wound you took
On my behalf
And on that day
I descended with my brothers
You were not there with us
And now I wait to find you
Now I wait for you
My spirit sings the rhythm
Of the beating of your heart

At the End of Jacob's Ladder

My shadow once encamped
Around you
From North to South
From East to West
I was with you always
I surrounded you
Snow fell
Waters rose
The sun tormented
The surface of your marble skin
In your eyes
The great I Am
Reflections of Fire
Clouds and Winds
And I encircled you
Again and again
And I slept at the pedestal
Your feet were mounted upon
Sigils encrusted upon your feet
Through heat and through cold
Through Spring and through Fall
I was there
I blanketed
Your perfectly chiseled skin
Pure marble
Swathed by my fur
As the storms blew

I was steadfast
There, my head bowed
In front of your looming presence
Tempests raged
I left you not
I am your wolf
And you are my Archangel

You descended the ladder
With your brothers who surrounded you

I watched my soul
Leap from me and
Leave this place
And now I roam,
The scent of your blue blood
Running through your veins
Calls me home
To you
Just a minute now
And I will be
With you again

C. JoyBell C.

My Brothers

I thought he was trying to drown me
Holding onto my ankle
I couldn't reach the air
I could see the sunlight
Dancing on the top of
The mercurial water
The light reached down to me
I wanted to scream out to it
So it would form hands and
Grab my arms
Pull me up to the surface
But
He was holding onto my ankle
I couldn't believe it
He was trying to kill me!
And just a minute ago I was
Admiring his perfectly sculpted
Intricately honed
God-form
While he lurked beside the pool
The sky was
Silver like the silvery pool of water
I couldn't possibly tell if it was
Morning or afternoon or evening
I think the sky was always that way
The sunlight was just caught in between
The argent sky and the pool of mercury
So I had the feeling there was no time
That nothing changed in that place

They were perfect
They were beautiful
Beautiful forms, breathtaking
They loitered the edges of the pool
With their flawless bodies
Like marble, like living marble
I jumped into the pool
To catch their attention
For some reason
My humanity embarrassed me
I felt like I was
Too infatuated with the humans
And that they
Were not contaminated with
The same human emotions
That infected me
And now, just my luck
One of them was trying to kill me
I was going to die there, that way
By drowning
A god was drowning me
He held me down in the water
Placed my feet onto the very bottom
My skin felt the rough surface of
The bottom of the pool
And now I was so far away from the air
I needed to survive
I was going to die, I could feel it
But right before I broke the surface
I inhaled!
That involuntary inhale

C. JoyBell C.

You make
When you can't not breathe
Anymore
The mercury flooded my lungs
Silver water flooded my lungs and
I breathed it in like air
Just like air
There was no difference

Then I woke up
My bed was soaked in liquid silver
I knew it was more
Than just a dream
He wasn't trying to drown me
He was just reminding me
That I too, could breathe mercury
He was reminding me
Of all my brothers

We Are One

We are the bond
Of the Sapphire Sun
Bound by the One
Who binds all of Creation
United in blood
And umbilical chains
No distance can measure
Nor time comprehend
No space can come between
The brethren
The bond of the
Sapphire Sun
We howl at the Blue Moon
We call to the Sapphire Sun
No man that walks
Nor has ever walked this land
Dare intervene
This dynasty we bear
Pledged to the Archangels
Imprinted on the hearts
Of Angels
We are the guardians of the Moon
We are the gates of the Sun

C. JoyBell C.

Skellig Michael

Those rocks have been climbed
By these hands before
We laughed as we climbed
This precipice
We rejoiced together
And we jumped
From crevice to stone
From stone to step
From step to rune-marked tombstone
And the gulls laughed with us
They joined in our laughter
Until we could no longer breathe!
This place of wild abandon
This mount of jagged madness
Where people emerge from rocky cliffs
And souls abound on rune-embedded caskets
I saw the quiet woman
With bottomless eyes
Row her boat ten leagues around us
Without stopping to catch her breath
People with bottomless eyes
And laughter like gulls
Emerging from inscriptions upon stones
And grey mists cast by ocean waves
What is this crazed, drunken place?
Let's stay here

Wizards

He used to look at the photos on his wall
Photos of him and other things, too
He would stare and
Wait for everyone in the pictures
To move
They would begin to smile
They would begin to laugh
The trees would begin to sway in the winds
In the picture frames
Hanging on his wall

It was his secret
Something he told no one
No one but her
Because she was just like him
She too
Watched herself smile back at her,
Watched winds in picture frames
Push the grass and pick up the leaves

They would stare until
Fear overcame them
And they could gaze no more
They made things move
Or maybe they just saw things move
On the other side
Of reality

C. JoyBell C.

They were the only two people
They knew who could do that
So it felt like
They were the same
Like they were meant
To stay together

Wizards (2)

Do you remember the day
I turned that wasteland
Into a red rose garden?
Tell me why
Tell me how
Tell me
Talk to me
How did I do it?
Can you do that too?

I Know You

People, you know, they ask for so much
Sometimes, actually, a lot of the time
They write down lists
One, two, three, four, five
He should be this and that
Or that and this
She should fit this mold
And make me feel that way
And sometimes this way
He must bring me to the moon and back
Every single time we make love
She must know all the right words to say
To sooth my insecurities
To make me feel like WOW
And here I am
Not having a list
I just want that feeling
That I know him
And that he knows me
Do you understand what I mean?
I want him to look at me and when he does
I want to feel he knows
That he knows me
I want to feel that he's on my side
And always will be
And I want to be able to look at him and say
"I know you too."
That's it!
I just want to know and be known!

I Am Thea

I am not afraid
Of the demons that lurk
In the shadows of the waning moon
As she wanes and loses her glow
The demons emerge
And I will continue to feed
On my figs and honey
Because I am unafraid
I am not afraid to walk
Into the darkness, into the night
They do not scare me
Because they know me, they recognize
What I am, Who I am
I am not afraid
To wield my sword
To walk on the path where serpents
Are coiled in every corner
Under every root
Some are red, others yellow
Some vipers are black, others brown
I have been to the swamp of vipers
I have been to their pools, their murky waters
They hide in the mosses
That hang from willow trees
The very ground
Slithers and shakes
But I am not afraid!
They cannot harm me
They dare not show their fangs to me

C. JoyBell C.

They let me walk on top of them
These are long-abandoned places
I am led through these paths
Through the pools and the mosses
So that I may know the way through
And so they may honor me
They smell the blood in my veins
They recognize the inscriptions
On the palms of my hands
The Fingerprints on my skin
Imprinted by the hands that made me
When I walk through the Valley of Death
All of Death runs away from me
A table is prepared for me
In the presence of mine enemies
I feast on figs and honey

I Love You

Let me love you
And I will love you
Not only with the heartbeat
Inside of me
But I will love you with the heartbeat
Of the earth, the trees, animals
I will gather the pulses of all that live
Everything that beats
And mold it with my fingers
Into a love for you
And I will sculpt the outline of your face
Into the clay within my hands
Kneeling here
In the ground
Dirt on my knees
I will mold and I will sculpt,
The drops of me will fall out
And into this clay
I will make a love for you
So real
That the whole world and all the people
Will appear fake
In the light of it
And you will say to me
"Let the world fade away
Let's lock ourselves within this clay

C. JoyBell C.

        Let's bury our bodies
          Inside this clay
       Hands clasped together
            Your head
Tilted and pressed into my chest
My cheek pressed upon your hair
        We will turn to dust
            Together
And then our dusts will mingle
       Until we have truly
         Become one"

    You will love me that way
           And I you

I Love You Forever

Buried within clay
Inside this wooden casket
Our dusts mingle
Here, together
And all the sounds of
The world have gone
Only the frequencies
Of our vibrating souls
Beat within each
And every one of our dusts
Here, together
Under this ground
Enclosed by this clay
And wood
We still sing a song
We dance a dance
That becomes the hymn
Of the centuries
A love song sung
Of the strings and things
Of our meanings
And our purposes
Sewn and threaded
Within the remnants of our
Forgotten DNA
Oh how we crumbled together

C. JoyBell C.

Here, together
And mix together
In this casket like this

You have loved me forever
And I you

The Hum of the Tides

Cast me fast against that rock
Lay me on top of it
And spread me open

You will feel the winds
Move in you on that night
When I open you fully

The air will be cold
Against my skin
My skin will feel bumpy with chill

And I will run my fingernail
Over your cold skin
Sing for me now

My hum would be soft
The murmur of an ocean's tide
Gently lapping at the bay

But I would turn your gentle hum
Into a tumultuous roar
Even the lions will know my name

I will feel the winds in me
That night

Wide open

But more than that
You will be full of me
No room for anything more

Song of the Seagulls

You would pull me into you
And watch me dance
Atop your open self

I would pull you into me
To watch you
Move inside my open self

We would move as one
Until the stars
Fall from the Heavens

We would be
Inside and inside and inside
One another

Until the Heavens come
To an end
Until demons become angels again

The rhythm of you
Inside me
Enough to cast waves against rocks

C. JoyBell C.

Over and over I
Would thrust myself
Into your open flesh

Until my song would be heard
By the seagulls
And they would imitate me

The seagulls would begin to sing your song
Sung into the skies
Breaking from your lips

With each thrust
I make
Inside of you

With each thrust
You make
Me hum

Inside Me

I called your name out
Into the fire
Into the fire
Of my solace
And my constant, agonizing, relentless
Desires
Into the night
And into the day
Your name resounded on
My lips
Only your name and the taste of
Your skin
My lips have bore
Every day Every day
The dampness of your pores
On my tongue
Remind me of
Things that I
Wish to whisper
Into your ear
While you move inside of me

C. JoyBell C.

Scratches on Your Back

The best state to be in
Is this state of being
Spread out open
For you
Just for you
This state
When all my tongue wants to do
Is lick.
Lick the contours of your arm
While your fingers
Do wonders inside of me
I want to lick all the way
From your wrist
Up to your shoulder
Feeling the every curve
Of your muscles
And veins
On the surface of my wet tongue
And then the bite comes
I bite your neck
And smell the scent of your hair
And goosebumps on your skin
I bite into you
Because you make me moan

Scratches on your back

What I Deserve

I deserve to be loved
Deeply
Until I am ashes restless in the earth
Until my soul has returned and left again
A hundred times over
Until you and I have forgotten
That there is such a thing, somewhere
They call "time"

And I deserve to be fucked
Deeply
Until your ears know nothing
But the sound of my cries
Until your mind remembers nothing
But the throbbing of my insides
Fuck me deeply
Until you and I forget
That there is such a thing, somewhere
They call "breathing"

C. JoyBell C.

What it Means

I don't care what they say
I want every thrust you make
In me
To mean that you love me

I don't care what they want
I want every moan I make
Every sigh
To become the hymn that
Your soul will memorize

I want the way I call out your
Name
To become the hymn, the pledge
Of your heart and mind

And I want every thrust
You make inside me
To remind me
Time and time again
Of just how much you
Love me

I don't care what they want
I don't think about what they
Say or believe
This is what I want to know
This is what I want to have

This is what it means

The Neighbors Know Your Name By Now

The wind blows strong
Casting young avocados from the avocado tree
Onto the tin roof
One after the other they hit the
Roof above us like bullets
Or hand grenades
The cool wind
Blowing through the window
Seems to rock me like a lullaby
And I'm here, held tight in your arms
In between my legs is sore
But feels so good
You kiss me while you
Move in me
And I like being transfixed into your eyes
All I can see in them, is the reflection
Of me
But how you feel inside me
Makes me close my eyes
And call out your name
Your thumb on my cheek
Says so many things, feels like so many things
You hold my face to yours
You won't let me out of sight
You won't stop moving in between me
You just won't stop making love to me
Every pore in me dilates

C. JoyBell C.

Beads of sweat are born
I can't contain myself
The neighbors know your name by now
You just won't stop fucking me
And there is no bed
There are no sheets
All that holds me in place
Is your arm around my back, underneath me
And your hand on my face
Keeping me right where you want me
Keeping me from writhing
From kicking you off of the bed!
And you're still moving inside me
In between my legs
You're still pushing me so open
Over and over
I feel so stretched and penetrated
I'm so sore but
You feel so good, I could die
The taste of your skin on my tongue
Is the only thing holding me
Onto this planet

Breakfast

Breakfast consists of
Me with my panties down
Lying on my back
On top of our dining room table
First it starts with me
Sitting on the edge
My nightgown pulled up my thigh
Your fingers skimming down my legs
Pulling down my panties
And then you spread me open
On the edge of the table
The earth quakes
And I'm sure that
A thousand birds take flight
Somewhere in China
When your lips reach my lips
Down there
I can't take it anymore
I can feel your tongue now
I have to lie down on the table
Pull on your shirt
Make you take your pants off
And make love to me
Push your hardness into me
That's how I like breakfast

C. JoyBell C.

Unholy Places

I don't want to be untouched
Undiscovered and unknown
I don't want to be virgin
I want your endless fingers
To unfold me, to run
In and out
Of me

I don't want to be pure
Sanctified and secret
I don't want to be hidden
I want myself open
Your tongue knowing the taste
The texture
Of me

I don't want to be dignified
Applauded and hailed
I don't want to be canonized
I want you to bend me over
Press me down
And eat every unholy place
On me

Our Darkness

We have a darkness
And a light
All our own

Our light feels like
Answers to my
Deepest, oldest prayers

Our light feels like
Being swathed in silk
Bathed in milk

But our darkness

Our darkness feels like
My breath being sucked
Out of my lungs

Our darkness feels like
Hot coals
On my stomach

Oh god, our darkness

It feels like
The tips of all my nerves
On fire

C. JoyBell C.

It feels like
The center of me
Being sucked on

Oh yes, our darkness

I would crawl
On all fours
To feed on this

I am
Naked, naked, naked
To know this

In and out
From the outside in
To the inside out

I can smell you
All over my skin
Your tongue clings to me

Your Fingerprints

There is something about
Your fingers
Why I want them inside me
So, so bad
You see,
With our hands
We take in what we need
We hold onto
All that we wish to keep
We grasp onto
Cling to
The things we never want
To let go of
That's how you make me feel
When you push
Your fingers
In between me
I feel like
The one thing you never
Ever want to let go of

I want your fingerprints
Inside me

All the way in

C. JoyBell C.

This Will Never End

Is there anything better
In existence?
Anything better than
Being pinned
Onto this bed
Feeling your sweat
Drip onto my back
And the texture
Of the bedsheet
On my tongue and lips?

Biting into the sheets
As your sweat
Trickles up my spine
My knees nearly raw
Your fingers through my hair
So gentle, so soft

So hard and so true
Is the rhythm that ripples
Through my backbone
And vibrates down my thighs

Your reassuring voice
Telling me how good it feels
To be inside me

And I think this just might never end

I Have a Sin

I have a very sinful thought
A sinfully dirty desire
And I never thought that I
Would want this
Would feel this
For someone
For any man
So I feel myself
Hiding in the shadows
Of myself
Just so I don't have to
Face the truth of my desires
Because this need I have
This yearning inside of me
Is just too dirty

I want
To take your fullness
Into my mouth
Grab onto your hipbones
And move you
In and out
Over my tongue
Until you moan
Until you grab my hair
And look me in the eyes
To see me filled with you
And your lips redden
And the arteries in your neck

C. JoyBell C.

Pulsate with ecstasy
I want to move you in and out
Over my tongue
In between my lips
Until it makes me moan
And you reach for my legs
And beg to make love to me

New Orleans

I have seen a wickedness
Right here in New Orleans
I didn't mean to
And maybe now I will need
To visit a Priest
Who will pray for me
And sprinkle me
With Holy Water
I didn't mean
To see what I saw
She was just standing there
On steps covered in Blue Moon Wisteria
When he lifted her dress,
Gathered it into a knot at her waist,
And licked in between her legs!
She moaned and
I should have run away!
But instead I hid behind the fountain
And watched him on his knees
Pressing his mouth into her lips
Licking and licking and licking
Her clit
He stroked her thigh
I think she was trembling
And I think I was trembling too
The air was a little cold
And his two fingers went
Inside her
I need to visit a confessional
Forgive me father, for I have sinned

C. JoyBell C.

Places of Sin

I know that I promised to find you again
And I know this because
I have found all my forgotten things
Inside you
All the things and parts
That I left inside you for safe keeping
And I think this is why
I did that
So that I would know it was you
When I found you again
My new eyes wouldn't be able to recognize you
I knew that
My new mind wouldn't be able to
Remember your name
I knew that
But I knew my soul would
Be able to recognize
Its secrets
So I left my secrets
Inside you
And I know that it's you
Because in you I've
Found my secrets again
All hidden inside you
All wrapped up inside you
You tell them to me
When you talk to me
You remind me
When I hear your voice

You say the same exact things
Sometimes
Do you realize that?
So because I know that it's you
I invite you into me
Body and soul
I ask you to consume me
Like the only food you've
Ever eaten
I ask you to
Own me like
I'm the only thing you have ever
Wanted
And will ever, ever
Want
I ask you to
Make love to me
In all the ways I know you want to
I want you to
Fuck me
In all the ways you know I like it
These secrets
Are not just of the soul
But these secrets
Are also of the treasured
Unholy places
Of our bodies
Sacred places of sin
My favorite places, really

The wet places

*"Far and near, they surround us, and, although
of immortal essence, they assume ever-changing forms,
according to nation, epoch, or region...
I struggled to find them, braved death, and,
as is said, descended into hell to
tame the demons of the abyss, to
summon the gods from on high to my
beloved Greece, that lofty heaven might
unite with earth, listening with delight
to strains divine.*

*Celestial beauty will become incarnate
in the flesh of woman,
the Fire of Zeus will run
in the blood of heroes, and,
long before mounting to the constellations,
the sons of God will shine forth like immortals."*

~ *Orpheus*

Ciao ciao! ♡

The Making of the Book Cover:

    I knew this was going to be my most ambitious book cover to date.

    I first worked with Corinne Knapp Rogers, owner of Hampton Photography NY, on the cover of my other book, *All Things Lit Like Fireflies*. She was truly a joy to work with, as her professionalism, eagerness, and entrepreneurial spirit really did shine through during every step of the way. Prior to meeting Ms. Rogers, the book cover design stages of my book-creating and publishing journeys were always stressful on my part. I would have to repeatedly convince photographers that getting themselves out there as the cover of a book is good exposure for them and an excellent platform to showcase their work! What better way to expand your horizons than by creating book covers for literature? Discovering Ms. Rogers was a totally positive experience for me. Corinne is an entrepreneur at heart and marketing is in her veins! I can honestly appreciate that very much, since I have to think just like that, myself being an independent author who is responsible for every angle of my own creations— from the thought-seed conception to the final product on those bookshelves. Her spark caught with my spark and the resulting flare was bright, newborn and unstoppable! I am very thankful to have found such a professional and commendable person to work with. I really couldn't have asked for more!

For the cover of *Wolves of the Sapphire Sun*, the idea was to create a frontline atmosphere to be the face of the collective story that the gist of the poems in this book are telling. I wanted to put a face on the archangel incarnate, the wolf that she is bound to, whilst not leaving out the voice and the whispers of the half-witches and the wizards! The spells and the incantations! And of course, the wildness! Oh, the wildness! Alas, the seemingly disparate characters in this book, all boil down to the embodiment of just two— two lovers.

I messaged Corinne and said, "Do you have a wolf we can work with?" Of course, people don't just "have wolves," but as serendipity would have it, Corinne's sister-in-law, Margaret Duffy, is a dog groomer who happens to have a loyal patronage of— you guessed it— dogs who look like wolves! And there you have it! The serendipitous sweetness of things playing at her finest!

The day of the shoot was cold, frigid; there was snow on the ground! This was only shortly after the polar vortex cyclones swept through the United States and froze Niagara Falls right in her tracks! There were three girls who modeled for the part that day, namely, Corrie-Ann Knapp, Danielle Porcella and Savonna Sanzeri. It was so cold; they had to wear thick leggings underneath their costumes (the beautiful gowns). Yet they made it look like the snow was warm frosting! I just have to commend all three of them on being such true troopers!

Initially, the photoshoot was set to take place at the Bird Sanctuary off Cross Bay Blvd. in Broad Channel, Queens, New York City; but then the security guard there asked them to leave (thanks for just doing your job, Mr. Security Guard of Bird Sanctuary in Queens, but you missed out on seeing three beautiful women in beautiful dresses, having an incredible photoshoot), so they found a new location behind the town's football field! And that's where our magic was brewed! Danielle, Corrie-Ann and Savonna were each shot for an hour, amounting to a thousand photos en totale!

Yukon's Frank Bassetti was there the whole time, rewarding our alpha with some steak he had tucked into a sandwich bag in his pocket! Extra treats for Yukon for being so amiable to work with!

I asked Corinne, "I really hope you weren't scared when the security guard kicked you out of the Bird Sanctuary!" and she said to me, "No, we weren't scared! We had a LOT of fun!" And I thought, "That's my girls!" And then I thought, "Spoken like a true New Yorker!"

And now for the cast and crew...

Corinne Knapp Rogers, our "book cover planner du jour", is the mother of four boys and the owner of Hampton Photography NY. She credits her love of photography to her very first love, her firstborn, Tyler, who is now seventeen years old (in a month). She also has Noah, who will be fifteen also in a month, thirteen-year-old Gavin and her youngest is Ronnie, now two-years-old. When asked about her most difficult time in life, she says that would definitely go to her divorce in 2009 and to the loss of her twenty-two-year-old baby brother, Joseph Knapp, eight years ago. "My heart still breaks every day, for the loss of him" she says. And when she says this, her pain is palpable. "But I met my fiancé in 2010, I'm happy now and life goes on... but my brother... will you please mention him in the book? That would make me and my whole family so happy." She didn't know that I had already written his name down, right after I heard about him.

Corinne was born and raised in Queens, NYC, in a town called Broad Channel, where she grew up on Rockaway

Beach. The only time she moved away from the ocean, was when she got married and lived with her then husband in Western Mass, Massachusetts, in a town called Warren. I asked her, "What is your favorite thing in the world?" and she said, "The ocean! Even though I live in the Hamptons area of Long Island now, I find myself driving to Queens to go to my home— Rockaway Beach! So many great times and memories for me there, it's the place where I feel most peaceful." I liked hearing that last part, that "…it's the place where I feel most peaceful" part. For some reason, those words agreed with me and sunk in, too. I think we all look for the place where we feel the most peaceful and we all call it our favourite thing. But of course I had to ask what her favourite perfume is (that's just me being me) "I'm wearing Donna Karan Cashmere Mist right now! But my fav is Calyx, probably been using it since I was sixteen!" And then I asked her, "Do you think you've found your soul mate?" and she said, "You know, I really might have! But I'm trying to find myself first… it's been a hard few years for me." And on that note, I thought, *It's usually been a hard few years, for too many of us.* But then I remembered how she said, "I'm happy now and life goes on!" and that just makes all the difference. Makes the feeling in my soul go from falling to flying!

Joseph Knapp, if you're seeing this right now, know that we all hope you are flying around wild and free somewhere in the sky.

www.hamptonphotographyNY.com

Yukon, with proud owner, Frank Bassetti.

Yukon became a part of the Bassetti family in Wintertime, November of 2006 when he was only nine-weeks-old and weighed just eleven pounds. Shortly after leaving the shelter where he was adopted from, Yukon faced a life-or-death situation after being seriously infected with parvovirus. His new family had to accept the possibility of losing their newest member just a week after welcoming him into their arms. Yukon though, staying true to the fighter in him, after just two weeks in the hospital, was strong and well enough to come home! Frank says, "We wanted a big dog but didn't expect Yukon to grow to a hundred and twenty pounds and be taller than the kitchen table!"

When I saw Yukon for the first time, I didn't need to dwell upon his appearance for even a moment. He was exactly as I envisioned him to be, it's like I  had already known him and ran with him long distances! He had strength, an inner pull; and yet he possessed an ethereal lightness of being.

Being a Tamaskan— a breed of dog native to Finland and closely related to lupines and known for their notable lupine appearance and nature— most people do find his size and wolf-like features to be intimidating; but once anyone gets to know him it's not long before they realize that he really is a gentle giant who likes to spend most of the day in the backyard, going out for long walks and chewing on a very good bone!

"He really is a great family dog, except for the time he ate the couch! We are still pissed about that." Says Frank.

"Laughter is timeless, imagination has no age and dreams are forever. Walt Disney said that. I'm a big Disney fan, I always loved Disney." Says Savonna, who in fact reminds me of Disney's Snow White. The thing that strikes me most about my Muse, is her desire to talk about everyone but herself. She bubbles over like a fountain when talking about

the people who are close to her heart; but can't seem to think of anything to talk about when it comes to herself. She loves deeply and truly. That is how I see it. "I go to St. Edmund Prep High School and I have three best friends; Patricia Magliaro, Jamie Siller and Brittany McGovern. My best friends are really important to me because without them I don't know what I would do. They've been my best friends for as long as I can remember. They're the kind of friends that I'll grow old with. Patricia sings... and she sings amazingly! I always wanted to be a singer, too, but now with University ahead of me, I'm not very sure what exactly I'm going to do. Jamie is probably the best artist I've ever known about, hahha, and Brittany is just crazy! She's a red head... I call her "ging" but I like her crazy because everyone needs a little crazy in their life!"

I listen to her and as I do, I feel pulled in to her world of friendship and value. The amount of value she gives to her friends is evidently more than what she gives to talking about herself. It makes me wonder about her life, her friendships, it makes me wish I had friendships like that when I was her age. "I live with my Aunt Jen because I loved her so much as a child. I still love her very much. She needed me and I needed her, so my mom let me live here in New York City with my Aunt Jen. When we came here from Florida, I was around four or five-years-old and now I'm eighteen and couldn't be more happy with my life here! Moving here completely changed me as a person because I have realized that if I stayed in Florida... I wouldn't have met all my friends and I wouldn't be with Aunt Jen. Who knows how I would have turned out if I stayed in Florida! Probably wouldn't have had the education that I have now... I wouldn't have anything that I have now. My Aunt Jen and I are a team. She will always and forever be *my heart*. She tells me that all the time and it's true." With these words I begin to paint a picture in my mind of a girl deeply in love with the people who matter to her, a girl in love with New York City and all that this city represents for her and has become for her... I also spent *my* formative years in Florida, after spending my earlier childhood in Baltimore, Maryland. And I remember my first visit to NYC, very well! My parents were terrified, they were convinced it was the city of sin and death, they locked all the doors in the car and told me not to stick my head out the window! Of course, I still stuck my head out the window to behold people with pink and blue hair! "Punk heads!" my dad said. "Magic!" I thought. So I ask her why she moved to NYC; "My mom wanted a better life for me and my dad left us." And I thought, *Aaaahh, yes, the loving mother who only wants what's best for her daughter.*

When I look at Savonna's photos with Yukon, I see a girl and a wolf bonded. I think this is especially enhanced by the shot wherein they're attached at the side but looking down and in opposite directions— their body language conveys a distance, a time and maybe even lifetimes apart. And yet they are bonded at one another's sides. The emotion, the vibration— is subtly intense and continuous. "Everyone at the photoshoot noticed how much Yukon liked me," she says. And I tell her, "You know I believed in you from the very first moment I laid eyes on you, right? I think this is your destiny." And she says to me, "I too, think this is my destiny."

Beyond her chemistry with Yukon that is so evident in the photos— Savonna has an aura which I can see and feel. And it is this countenance, which convinces me that she is my Filippa, that she effortlessly portrays the thought of this book.

But of course I need to ask her the most important question of all, "What perfume do you love?" "Tommy Girl perfume!" she answers. "I also like turtles. My Aunt Jen's best friend, Jenny Albert, worked at Sea World saving turtles. Her and I were very close but she's already passed away. She was always so sick, always in and out of the hospital… but anyway, that's why I like turtles. I also love the colour purple! My room is purple, even the colour of my school is purple! And I like playing soccer." I wonder what her heritage is, as she could very well be anything from Italian to Eurasian! "I'm mostly Italian, I know that I'm also part German but I really don't know my whole story for sure. I could be anything because whenever I ask anyone about my heritage, they always tell me so many different things! So I could be anything, really! Who knows?" Furthermore, she says, "I don't really do much, my life isn't so exciting." And in these moments I feel like she has only overlooked everything that I see in her; for how exciting it is to love your friends and family truly, to be someone's "heart" and to know that they are your "heart" too, and to live in New York City! Oh, and also, to love the colour purple!

"I want you to know that from now on, I will see you as my sister," I told her, "If you ever need someone to talk to, you have me. I wish I had someone to talk to when I was your age, because I really didn't. But that's a different story…"

"It's nice to know I have you now. I really appreciate that. I don't really have anyone to talk to now either… I don't have any siblings so it's nice that you think of me as a sister. You're a sister to me now, too."

The main typeface in this book is set in 12 pt. *Perpetua*, by Eric Gill (1882- 1940) who was a British sculptor and stonecutter named *Royal Designer for Industry* by the *Royal Society of Arts* in London. The font itself was made to resemble hand-chiseled engravings, hence, who better to create such a feel for a font, than a sculptor and stonecutter?

"Perpetua may be judged in the small sizes to have achieved the object of providing a distinguished form for a distinguished text; and, in the large sizes, a noble, monumental appearance."
~ Stanley Morison

Notes...

Notes...

Made in the USA
San Bernardino, CA
11 January 2015